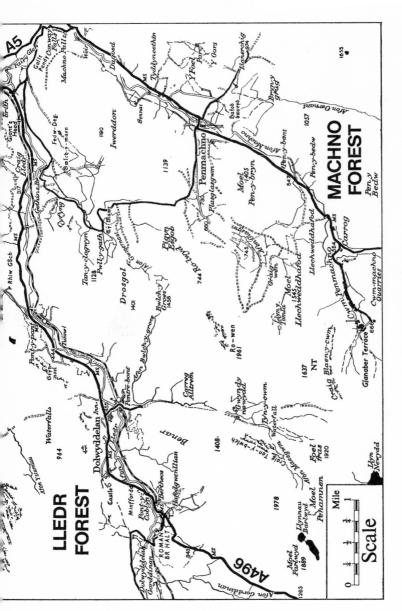

The Gwydyr Country in 1920.

**DARTINGTON AMENITY RESEARCH TRUST**
Central Office, Shinner's Bridge,
Dartington, Totnes, Devon.

The cover picture shows Moel Siabod and plantations in the Llugwy Valley, seen from an upland farmstead north of Betws-y-Coed.

Gwydyr Castle

FORESTRY COMMISSION BOOKLET No. 28

# GWYDYR FOREST IN SNOWDONIA

*A History*

By DONALD L. SHAW

*Forestry Commission*

*LONDON*

HER MAJESTY'S STATIONERY OFFICE

1971

# ACKNOWLEDGMENTS

The cover picture, showing Moel Siabod and the uplands above Betws-y-Coed, is by Mr. I. A. Anderson, the Forestry Commission's Principal Photographer.

Charles Tunnicliffe, R.A., of Bodorgan, Anglesey, drew the frontispiece showing Gwydyr Castle, and the views throughout the text.

Mr. C. R. Dick, the Commission's Chief Forester at Gwydyr, kindly provided eighteen of the black-and-white photographs. The eight exceptions are: Plates 4, 7, 17 and 18, by Mr. R. Thompson of Denbigh; Plates 8 and 21, by Mr. W. A. Poucher; Plate 14 from the Forestry Commission collection, reference D 2199; and Plate 19 by the Central Office of Information.

The maps are reproduced from the Ordnance Survey, by kind permission of the Director General.

SBN 11 710010 2

# FOREWORD

In 1920 the Forestry Commission began the transformation of a great expanse of steep hillside and moorland, around Betws-y-Coed in North Wales, into modern productive forest.

The few old oakwoods that remained, and the remarkable scenery of riverside, lake and crag, were treated with the consideration they merited when spruce, larch, pine and Douglas fir were brought in. In 1937 the Forestry Commission, to encourage wider public access to the woods and hills, embodied this young Gwydyr Forest into its Snowdonia Forest Park, which became encircled some ten years later, by the larger Snowdonia National Park of the Countryside Commission.

Today, the original Gwydyr Forest, named after historic Gwydyr Castle near Llanrwst, forms three management units. Lledr Forest and Machno Forest, each called after the valley it occupies, have been hived-off as they reached timber-yielding stature.

Early in this new woodland's history, Mr. J. L. Shaw took charge of its planting and development. His son Donald, the author of this present booklet, was brought up in the heart of the forest, where he too now serves. He has thus had a long and unique connection with the woods he describes with such deep understanding.

As time goes on, few people remain who can appreciate the long struggle to change bare moors into thriving woodlands. Here at Gwydyr this has been accompanied by a steady decline of the marginal hill farms, the lead mines and the slate quarries. Forestry, by producing steady employment and creating magnificent scenery to sustain the growing tourist industry, has ensured continuous employment in this loveliest region of Caernarvonshire.

So this sympathetic record of the toil and slow triumph of the foresters, who built up the Gwydyr woods over the years, has been put into print. It appears just fifty years after the work began, as the first trees attain full stature. Gwydyr's future will be one of continuous forest cover, with replanting filling in the gaps where mature trees are felled for timber.

This booklet aims to give, to the many appreciative visitors, a fuller understanding of all that forestry means to the uplands of North Wales, and to their people.

FORESTRY COMMISSION,

25 Savile Row,

London W1X 2AY.

*May* 1970

v

# CONTENTS

vii

Llanrwst Bridge

## Chapter 1

# THE FOREST BACKGROUND

## 1 – HISTORICAL NOTES

> Love had he found in huts where poor men lie;
> His daily teachers had been woods and rills,
> The silence that is in the starry sky.
> The sleep that is among the lonely hills.
>
> *Wm. Wordsworth*

### THE WYNNS OF GWYDYR

Much of Gwydyr Forest bestrides historic land so we should secure a brief glimpse of the famous Wynn family, who contributed so much to its history. Unfortunately, few records remain for a comprehensive memoir, and much that we do know has been contributed by Sir John Wynn, the historian of the family.

Sir John was born in 1553. His character has aroused controversy – many held him to be all that was worthy and prudent; others describe him as signifying craftiness and arrogance. Perhaps his true character lay somewhere in between, and in his contrasting emotions aroused by the vicissitudes, treachery and turbulence of his times. Certainly he must have been talented – he was made Member of Parliament for the county of Caernarvon in 1596, a member of the Council of the Marches of Wales and created a baronet in 1611.

Shrewd and successful in various ventures, his critics tended to believe he oppressed his fellow men . . . Yorke (in his *Royal Tribes of Wales*) comments: 'It is the superstition of Llanrwst to this day, that the spirit of the old gentleman lies under the great waterfall "Rhaiader y Wennol" (Swallow Falls), there to be punished, purged, spouted upon and purified from the foul deeds done in his days of nature'. Evidently he was a man who essayed to make the best of two worlds. When, in 1615, Sir John – having incurred the displeasure of the Council of the Marches, who appealed to Lord Ellesmere, then Chancellor – made his peace in the surest manner by paying a bribe of £350 to square the court and retain his name on the Commission for Caernarvonshire, he immediately eased his conscience by founding a hospital, endowing a school at Llanrwst, and yielding up sundry tithes to support these charities. At the funeral of Henry, Prince of Wales, Sir John bore one of the great standards. His life appeared governed by an admixture of retirement and activity; among the principal interests with which he concerned himself were the reclamation of land along the Caernarvonshire coast (particularly the Tremadoc estuary), a survey of the mountains, and mining operations in Anglesey and in the hills west of Llanrwst, where Gwydyr Forest now stands. His clash with Bishop Morgan is something of a classic.

The controversy raged when the Bishop would not confirm a lease of church lands held by Sir John, and pleaded in a letter 'conscience', which he claimed 'asserteth me that your request is such that in granting it, I should prove myself an unhonest, unconscionable and irreligious man; ye, a sacrilegious robber of my church, a perfidious spoiler of my Diocese and an unnatural hinderer of preachers and good scholars, etc., etc.'

Vehement and condemnatory language indeed from a Bishop!

Sir John cared little for the charge of robbery and sacrilege, but he did care a very great deal for what he considered his lawful rights. An extract from his reply to the Bishop's letter emphasises his intolerance.

'The sower went out to sow and some of his seed fell in stony ground where it withered because it could take no root. The seed was good, but the land naught. I may justly say so by you. I have in all showed myself your friend, in so much as if I had not pointed you the way with my finger (whereof I have yet good testimony) you would had been still vicar of Llanrhayder. You plead conscience when you should give and make no bones to receive courtesy of your friends . . . but I appeal to Him that searcheth the conscience of all men, whether you have used me well and whether it be conscience (which you ever have in your mouth) be the sole hindrance of my request . . . I never expect goodwill of you, nor good turn by you.'

The baronet of Gwydyr evidently had very little veneration for the clerical office, although it seems doubtful if he ever got his lease of land confirmed after these spiteful exchanges of correspondence.

Sir John's curious attitude to churchmen can be taken a stage further when we consider his directives to his chaplain at Gwydyr on his manner of life and behaviour. The poor man is counselled and directed thus:

'You shall have the chamber I showed you in my gate (a gloomy room in the extreme) private to yourself, with lock and key and all necessities. In the morning I expect you to say prayers in my hall, to my household below, before they go to work and when they come in at nights. I beg you to continue for the more part in the lower house; there is a bailiff of husbandry and a porter who will be commanded by you.

'Before dinner you are to come up and attend grace or prayers. When the table, from half downwards, is taken up then are you to rise and to walk in the alleys near at hand until grace time, and then to come in for that purpose.

'After dinner, if I be weary you may go to bowls, shuffleboard or any other honest recreation; if I go riding I shall liken your company. I would have you go every Sunday in the year to some church hereabouts to preach, giving warning to the parish to bring the youths at afternoon to the church to be catechised; in which point is my greatest care that you be diligent.

'Avoid the alehouse . . . to sit and keep drunkards company there being the greatest discredit your function can have. . . .'

The memory of Meredith ap Ieuan – the founder of the family of Gwydyr – was commemorated by a brass in Dolwyddelan church. In the Gwydyr chapel there existed a marble tablet containing the following pedigree: (From a *History of the Wynn Family* by Sir John Wynn, 1st published in octavo 1770).

'This chapel was erected A.D. 1633 by Sir Richard Wynn of Gwydyr, in the county of Caernarvon, Kt. and baronet, treasurer to the high and mighty Princess Henrietta Maria, Queen of England, daughter of Henry IV, King of France, and wife of our sovereign King Charles. Where lyeth buried his father Sir John

3

Wynn of Gwydyr, Kt. and baronet, son and heir to Maurice Wynn, son and heir to John Wynn, son and heir to Meredith, which three lyeth buried in the church of Dolwyddelan, with tombs over them. This Meredith was son and heir to Evan, son and heir to Robert, son and heir to Meredith, son and heir to Howell, son and heir to David, son and heir to Griffith, son and heir to Caeradock, son and heir to Thomas, son and heir to Roderick lord of Anglesey, son to Owen Gwyneth, Prince of Wales and younger brother to David, Prince of Wales, who married E'me Plantagenet, sister to King Henry II.'

'There succeeded this David three princes; his nephew Leolenis Magnus, who married the daughter of King John; David, his son, nephew to King Henry III, and Leolyn – the last Prince of Wales of that line – who lived in King Edward I's time. Sir John Wynn married Sydney, who lieth buried here, the daughter of Sir William Gerrard Kt., lord chancellor of Ireland, by whom he had issue – Sir John Wynn, who died in Italy, Sir Richard Wynn, now living, Thomas Wynn, who lieth here, Owen Wynn, now living, Robert Wynn, who lieth here, Roger Wynn, who lieth here, William Wynn, now living, Maurice Wynn, now living, Ellis Wynn, who lieth buried at Whitford in the County of Flint, Henry Wynn, now living – and two daughters, Mary, now living and married to Sir Roger Mostyn in the County of Flint, and Elizabeth, married to Sir John Bodwill, in the County of Caernarvon.'

The Gwydyr Chapel was probably built from a design by Inigo Jones.

Local tradition has long asserted that Sir John Wynn was one of the first to obtain a hint of the existence of the Gunpowder Plot and that he did so through his cousin Dr. Thomas Williams of Trefriw, a zealous Roman Catholic. Presumably Dr. Williams sent the baronet an enigmatical letter foretelling some impending catastrophe, and recommending him to absent himself from Parliament. Sir John took the warning with him to London and there found a member who had received similar advice – from an anonymous source. A secret held by two became no secret at all, and as history confirms the Gunpowder Plot was discovered and frustrated. But Sir John, shrewdly, did not betray his knowledge and his kinsman's name was never disclosed to Protestant or Papist.

One interesting detail in the Wynn family history is its association with so celebrated a figure in Welsh chronicles as Catherine de Berain – 'Mam Gwalia' as she was popularly called.

Catherine had four husbands – the first Salisbury of Lleweni, the second Sir Richard Clough, the third Maurice Wynn of Gwydyr and her fourth Edward Thelwall. 'Mam Gwalia' is said to have been a singular character, but in what way her singularity is defined – assuming we overlook her quartet of marriages – is not altogether clear. We are told she lost little time in courting. After the funeral of her first husband she left the church in company with Maurice Wynn, who proposed to her. But he was graciously declined, being informed that he was just a little too late and that Sir Richard Clough had proposed to her and been accepted – as the funeral procession wended its way to the graveyard. However, 'Mam Gwalia' assured Maurice that in the event of there being 'another opening' he should surely be her third.

And he was.

The second Sir Richard Wynn's only daughter became the wife of Lord Willoughby, 1st Duke of Ancaster.

Sir John Wynn began building Upper Gwydyr (Gwydyr Uchaf) in 1604 and when completed it was considered one of the finest houses in the Principality. Apparently it was planned to receive any members of the Royal family who might have occasion to travel to Ireland, but more probably Upper Gwydyr house was destined for the reception of the Lords Deputies of Ireland, since it was not far from the London-Holyhead road (the present A.5). In 1610 Sir John erected some almshouses in Llanrwst (named Jesus Hospital) for the reception of twelve poor men. This charity was liberally endowed with the rectorial tithes of Eglwys Fach.

Sir John Wynn died in 1626, aged 73. A famous saying of his should have some significance for us all – 'Poverty soon forgets whence it be descended, for it is an ancient saying that there is no poverty but is descended of nobilitie, nor no nobilitie but is descended of beggarie'.

In 1636 Llanrwst bridge, over the river Conway, was completed by Sir Richard Wynn (son of Sir John), groom of the bedchamber to Charles I when Prince of Wales, and later appointed Treasurer to Queen Henrietta.

At an earlier period, during the War of the Roses, the Wynns supported Lancaster and after the Duke of York's estate in Denbighshire had been ransacked by Lancastrian supporters, the King sent the Earl of Pembroke to recover the property, and in the ensuing campaigns much of Nant Conway was put to the fire and sword. At this time this great fastness of forest, moor and mountain was defended by Dafydd ap Sienkin, a captain of the Lancastrian faction and an outlaw. Notoriously skilful at concealment, ap Sienkin adapted a cave on the huge bastion of Carreg y Gwalch – a towering crag above Gwydyr Castle – as his headquarters and made innumerable sorties from this hideout. His **prowess** with a bow was legendary; on one occasion an important document was to be signed in a room in Gwydyr Castle, and to signify his displeasure, ap Sienkin shot an arrow from the entrance of his cave, through the open window of the room, dashing the quill from the fingers of a signator's hand and piercing the document as it lay on the table. Warning indeed; though this seemed downright intimidation.

In those days much of the area abounded with dense woods and up at Yspytty Ifan – a lordship belonging to St. John of Jerusalem – the woods harboured gangs of cut-throats and robbers having the privilege of sanctuary. A twenty-mile radius was unsafe from the depredations of these bands of brigands, as the peculiar jurisdiction in the Yspytty area was not governed by the King's laws and there were many divisions among friends and bondmen in those days.

Gwydyr, it has been said, derives its name from 'gwy' (water) and 'tir' (land), –hence 'wet land', possibly an allusion to the low-lying Conway Valley pastures, still flooded occasionally. But it may come from 'gwaed-dir' (bloody land), an allusion to the ferocious battles fought in the area by Llywel Hen about the year 610. Cradock, however, in his Welsh Tours, states 'the word Gwedir is supposed to signify glass, and the Wynn family were the first in these parts to possess a house with glazed windows'.

A pearl was presented to Catherine, wife of Charles I, said to have been fished off Trefriw by a relative of Sir Richard Clough, and this pearl was for some time a conspicuous object in the Royal Crown. Pearl fisheries in those times seemed to have been quite productive in the river Conway and particularly at Trefriw.

TREFRIW SPA

This former famous spa in the little village of Trefriw claimed the strongest chalybeate waters used medicinally in Europe. The water was of exceptional merit as regards tonic and curative properties – rich in sulphur-iron and also containing quantities of sulphates of alumina, magnesia, soda and silica in best medicinal form. Moreover, the iron existing in its highly assimilable curative state is known as ferrous sulphate.

| | |
|---|---|
| 100–250 A.D. | Roman legions, stationed at nearby Caerhun, realised the medicinal value of the water. They tunnelled into the Allt Cae Coch mountain to obtain it as it bubbled from a rock fissure. |
| 1753 | Much used by local inhabitants to treat both humans and cattle. A landslide covered the entrance to the caves. |
| 1833 | Caves re-excavated. |

| 1863 | First Bath-house built by Lord Willoughby de Eresby. |
| 1873 | Present Bath-house erected. |
| 1908–1965 | The recommended maximum dose was two table-spoonfuls (due to exceptional strength). It was found practicable to bottle samples before exposure to light and air and to send them by post to patients. For nearly fifty years this had relieved suffering in many thousands of people, to whom the Spa treatment would not otherwise have been obtainable. |

## II – MINING

They are ghost mines now, with eerie outlines in the silver moonlight. Amidst the pine, spruce and larch plantations of the bleak plateau of Nant Bwlch yr Haiarn, are located the remnants of a dozen or so lead mines – from the derelict mill and engine houses of the major workings to the lonely trial level with its few rusted wires and stunted posts; from an outlay of thousands of pounds to an investment of perhaps fifty. Until a few years ago one could still come across a rotted boot, a rusty shovel, a discarded pick, in some old drift or level.

What manner of men were those who secured their 'take note', or document of possession, from the Gwydyr Estate and set out on the exposed area of heather and bilberry moor to dig speculatively, pick and hammer at rock and shale, sink trial shafts and excavate levels, all by hand and often in the foulest weather conditions? Many came from Cornwall and Scotland, but the majority from Llanrwst and Trefriw in the Conway valley. All were dedicated to the quest for lead, or zinc, urged on doubtless by the evidence of mining activities since Roman times.

Major workings became established and absorbed much available labour, but individual and small-group effort always went on during the principal period of activity, between 1850 and 1919, and again from 1950 to 1959.

The majority of these mines are found within some eight square miles from the north side of the river Llugwy, flanked on the east by the Conway valley and extending northwards to the Llyn Crafnant area. The romantic names of some of these mines are fascinating – Hafna, Gorlan Farchog, Pandora, Coed Coch, Klondike. Why so alien a title as Pandora in this corner of the Principality? And Klondike? Is there an association here with the fabulous gold rush in the Yukon?

The earliest evidence of mining operations appears to have been determined on rough grazing pasture near Coedmawr, a mile or so north-west of Betws-y-Coed. Old diggings here are associated with Roman mining trials on Bryn Elen (Elen's mound or hill); close by was a Roman road thought to have been constructed from Miner's Bridge over the Nant moorland northwards to Caerhun. Doubtless Roman mining here was limited and probably of brief duration, but even in those far distant days interested people realised the potential wealth hidden in the ground and were prepared to look for it. Furthermore, the location of their workings – near to a thoroughfare – implied a strategic and economic significance. At a much later date Sir John Wynn became interested in developing the mineral potential too. On October 1st 1625 he wrote to Sir Hugh Myddleton in London: 'I have lead ore on my grounds in great store and other minerals near my house, if it pleases you to come hither'. It was an appeal to Sir Hugh for advice in exploiting these minerals.

Just over two centuries later, John Williams in his book *Faunula Grustensis* – an outline of the natural contents of the parish of Llanrwst published in 1830 – recorded that 'lead mines abound in this place and have been dug for ages as there have been many relics found which proved that the Romans explored the bowels of the Nant'.

We can thus perceive the constant awareness of the presence of ores and the efforts made to find them over the span of centuries; no major assault by 1830 perhaps, but dispersed scrabblings and scratchings, awaiting the age of the machine to facilitate extraction and lighten the hard labour.

After 1850 came the establishment of most of the major mines. The ten principal mines were Llanrwst, Hafna, Parc, Cyffty, Gorlan Farchog, Pandora (alternatively called Eagle and Willoughby), where diamond-tipped drills were first used in 1926, Coed Mawr Pool, Aberllyn (zinc), Klondike and Coed Coch (sulphur worked in 1917 and again for a brief trial period during the 1939–45 war). Of this number only three were in any way active until the late 20's or early 30's – Coed Mawr Pool, Cyffty and Pandora. Parc mine received much later attention. At great cost the latest-type survey drillings were undertaken, most of the underground workings were restored and extended between 1950 and 1959, a new mill was constructed and there was a brief interlude of activity and animation. Alas, it ceased and the inevitable history of the mines-activity, abandonment, activity, abandonment – has repeated itself.

Before 1850 mining was speculative and inconclusive. The 'take-note' system was in existence then and had continued throughout

*Plate 1.* View north-east over Betws-y-Coed towards Clogwyn Cyrau, the Corner Crags. Note foresters' timber houses.

*Plate 2.* Rugged sky-line of Creigiau Gleision, or Blue Crags, above Llyn Crafnant Plantations.

*Plate 3.* Llyn Geirionydd and its plantations, cradled amid hills west of Llanrwst.

the latter half of the century and into this. Briefly, it was a three-year agreement, on a trial period, at the option of the lessee, to apply for a mining lease for the whole period of twenty-one years, from the Gwydyr Estate. Whilst the 'take-note' system remained valid no intrusion or interference to the property could be inflicted by outside parties.

The initial working was by one interested group – perhaps two or three men or a party of half a dozen – who set out with pick and shovel, and if successful in striking a lode that proved remunerative, eagerly sought out a further group with the necessary capital resources to develop. It was bitterly hard graft in an uncompromising environment of exposure and uncertainty.

The lodes were ascertained to run generally from south-west to north-east but they occupied fissures and faulty zones at the junction of sedimentary rocks with igneous rocks. This resulted in angular irregularities and the following of many a false trail by the speculative lessees. They struggled on, picking away, until either in despair or through the utter lack of resources, they were forced to abandon their quest. Evidence of their efforts and their 'run on a false trail' can be seen in the large numbers of trial excavations in all kinds of bizarre locations – the base of huge crags, lonely sites amid heather and gorse, on rock ledges, on the shores of lakes. Viewed today, all this minor effort seems futile and without plan, yet a hundred, seventy, sixty years ago, it reflected hope and anticipation to the individual or small group who slogged away to justify their 'take-note' lease. Only a few were fortunate in their explorations and subsequent ample financial aid.

The actual mining was a hard, laborious task. The best of the excavated ore lumps were hand picked out and selected, and were then crushed manually by a flat hammer roughly twelve inches by six against an iron screen or grid. This was then passed on to a cradle-suspended sieve where one man had to rock the cradle until the smaller particles passed through the sieve. Washing was the next process and the concentrates were then sent off to Chester for smelting.

A thirty-five foot diameter water wheel was in use in Cyffty mine for many years. When a donkey pump was installed at the end of the first world war it used a ton of coal every twenty-four hours and the coal was fetched from Llanrwst, three miles away, by horse and cart.

Around 1880, at this mine, a monthly wage of £4 to £5 was considered good for the hard work involved and twenty-five shillings a week was earned by the average miner as late as 1920. One or two picturesque lakes in the area were artificially extended and some

9

small reservoirs made, to provide water power for the plant in which the ore was crushed and concentrated.

There is an interesting ecological association between the Alpine cress (*Thalaspi alpestre*) and the waste places and old walls of the lead mines. It is found on selected sites associated with lead, silver and zinc mining, and is a useful indicator plant. By the end of the 1930's a high proportion of land round and about the lead mines had been planted by the Forestry Commission, and today much of the unique mining character of this area is concealed behind and between large blocks of coniferous forest. The world of jaw crushers, coarse and fine grizzlies, jigs, vanners, trommels, wiffley tables and biddles – technical names for mining equipment – has vanished. What of the scarred landscape, the piles of waste? Slowly, year by year, they are becoming cloaked by maturing pine and spruce; many small trial excavations lie unseen beneath heather and bilberry in the plantation depths, and the unwary wanderer must beware. Natural regeneration of birch, rowan and alder is progressively colonising the piles of waste; moss and lichen grow on the old walls, submerging the stark outlines under a grey-green cloak. And far up on the heather-clad slopes, scree and strewn boulder conceal the detritus of old trial levels.

A feverish way of life, an adventure, a hard toiling, speculation, misery, success, defeat –reflecting the eternal restlessness of man for quest and gain – is being slowly hidden by an attractive, irregular pattern of conifer foliage. Over the long deserted workings the wind mourns. There is the sensation of loneliness and timelessness, echoed by the mountain stream and the melancholy call of curlew over the remote wastes of the moorland.

Only the ghosts remain.

## PRODUCTION

*Aberllyn*   Black slates and felspathic ash. Highest proportion of zinc in the assays averaged 44%. Old workings are remarkable for the coatings of hydrozincite on the walls. At intervals between 1869 and 1904 some 2,500 tons of zinc ore were raised, containing from 29–44% of zinc. There was an output of 25 tons of lead between 1899 and 1904 (containing 78–80% of lead).

*Caecoch*   Near the chalybeate wells of Trefriw. Mining of pyrites, a naturally occurring sulphate of iron, and the only mine of its kind in Europe. Spoil and workings are still to be observed as a reminder of this unique mineral deposit. Royalties were paid to the Gwydyr Estate based on the shipment of ore and date from 1826.

Miner's Bridge across the Llugwy, Betws-y-Coed.

*Hafna*   Shales and felspathic ash of Bala age, with greenstone intrusive sill. Splendid samples of schiefer-spar have been found and cockscomb pyrites is also abundant. Some of the lead ore contained seven ounces of silver per ton. Sample records of production here run as follows:

| 1898 | 27 tons lead ore | 81% lead | 229 tons zinc ore | 42% zinc |
|------|------------------|----------|-------------------|----------|
| 1909 | 112 ,,  ,,  ,,   | 82% ,,   | 208 ,, ,, ,,      | 41% ,,   |
| 1913 | 74 ,,  ,,  ,,    | 80% ,,   | 389 ,, ,, ,,      | 40% ,,   |

# III – GEOLOGY, TOPOGRAPHY AND METEOROLOGY

LOCATION

The forest area is centred on the village of Betws-y-Coed in Caernarvonshire, and plantations sweep into four valleys and across the hills between them. Northwards, down the fertile Conway Valley, they invest the western slopes as far as Dolgarrog; there are detached units farther on, some as far removed as the outskirts of Colwyn Bay and Llandudno Junction. Westwards, flanking Telford's famous A5 London–Holyhead highway up the course of the Llugwy river, they stretch towards Capel Curig and clothe the lower slopes of Moel Siabod, south of the village. Southwards, through and beyond the lovely Lledr Valley, they add a picturesque beauty to the crags and boulder-clad hillsides, and south-eastwards they contribute dignity to the less rugged Machno Valley.

TOPOGRAPHY

Hill slopes are generally steep, boulder-clad, and characterised by rock outcrops which frequently create terraces of varying area. These slopes generally culminate in beetling crags, often striated. Scree zones are not numerous, and are dispersed for the most part throughout the northern blocks. The Machno Valley is smoother of outline and hill delineations are distinctively gentler.

The plateau land is a complex region – broken and undulating, with terraces, ridge formations and low lying frost hollows. This is particularly evident north of the Llugwy Valley. A series of charming lakes and reservoirs lie in hollows across this area.

ELEVATION

Sea level to over 1,800 feet, with a mean around 750 feet.

## GEOLOGY

Practically the whole of the forest is contained on Ordovician formations, mainly of slates, shales and grits. The southern portion is dominated by slates, as evinced by the presence of slate quarries at Rhos (Capel Curig), and Hafodlas (Betws-y-Coed), and in the parishes of Dolwyddelan and Cwm Penmachno. South of the Llugwy there is little evidence of lead working. To the north, across the Nant plateau, where igneous intrusions cut through the sediments, mineralisation of these intrusions has provided workable lead deposits. Volcanic extrusive lavas, ashes and tuffs of the Snowdon and Crafnant series are widespread. Iron-ores, interbedded with black shales and associated with sulphur, occur at Trefriw.

## SOILS

On the hillsides these are primarily reddish shale-loams of the podsolic group, often clayey as regards matrix, but mainly well drained and aerated. The valley bottoms are of fertile alluvium.

Mountain peats are frequent, often extensive and variable in depth. They include heather-moor, *Eriophorum*-moor and *Molinia*-moor associations. Deep fibrous peat can be found in places where clay has accumulated on terraces, and also in depressions between rock outcrops, where drainage has been severely impeded in the past.

## METEOROLOGY

Average rainfall varies from 45 inches on low ground to over 80 inches on the higher areas, i.e. Crafnant and Hafodgwenllian. Rainfall is erratic and any month can be unusually wet or dry. In 1925, 26 inches of rain fell in five days in the headwaters of the Eigiau, some two miles north-west of the forest boundary.

Snow can be heavy at elevations of over 700 feet. In 1938 an exceptional fall of wet snow caused considerable damage to plantations on the lower slopes, particularly to Douglas fir. Snowfall generally, however, is variable; in early December 1967 some 22 inches fell in forty-eight hours, being a blanket fall unaccompanied by any strong wind. This followed three mainly open winters.

Maritime influences – particularly from the north – exercise a generally moderating effect, and extremes of climate are the exception rather than the rule.

Spring frosts can often be damaging, particularly on the plateau lands and in sheltered, moist sites on the lower areas. Gales in wet weather do cause loss from the effect of windthrow on the more exposed, rock-strewn ground conditions with thin soils, and at the bottom of deep, draughty valleys in the south of the forest, wind exerts a limiting effect on tree growth.

All aspects are encountered due to the dip and strata of the rocks, though over the forest areas as a whole there is an emphasis to the south east. The smoother, longer slopes in the southern blocks tend to accent this rather more visibly than the harsher, rugged profiles of terrain north of the Llugwy Valley.

Over 75% of the plantation area is subject to an exposure factor of moderate to severe. This is contributed to by:

(a) The high proportion of plantations established on land at 500 feet or above.

(b) The presence of so much shallow, peaty soil on ridges and shelves.

(c) The consistent problem of adequate drainage of very difficult sites on plateau country.

(d) Sporadic 'channelled' valley winds on upper, boulder-strewn hill slopes.

Generally the mountains to the west minimise the full effect of prevailing south-westerlies, but there is one weak link in the chain – the notorious gap between Moel Siabod and the Glyders – through which the full effect of south-western gales has ingress to the western and central areas of the forest.

The vast extent of plantations established on the plateau lands is now largely self-sheltering however, and well-planned thinnings have so far helped to minimise any large scale windblow.

Llyn Bodgynydd Bach, looking towards Crimpiau Ridges.

## Chapter 2

# LAND ACQUISITION

"And he gave it for his opinion, that whoever could make two ears of corn
or two blades of grass, to grow upon a spot of land where only one grew
before, would deserve better of mankind and do more essential service to
his country, than the whole race of politicians put together."

*Jonathan Swift.*

In the year 1920 two of the newly-formed Forestry Commission's
land acquisition officers came to the Conway Valley. The reason
for their presence? To acquire hillsides for afforestation and re-
afforestation in accordance with the policy of the Forestry Act of
1919. Their destination? The Gwydyr Estate office at Gwydyr
Uchaf, near Llanrwst. Gwydyr – the historic home of the distinguished Wynn family, whose estate embraced wild moorland and
foothill terrain as well as attractive valley scenery. A family whose
historical account has been steeped in turbulence and altercation,

15

but whose traditions of courage and loyalty were incontestable. Furthermore they had been great benefactors to local inhabitants by setting up industries and providing amenities.

This is Wagnerian country – boulder clad, steep-sided slopes, towering bluffs and crags with their bases strewn with scree, broken plateau land, mountain streams, and rugged moorland stretching to the foothills of the Snowdon range – and in the musical interpretation best exemplified by fortissimo chords from brass and rolls from timpani. This is no country for the delicate scoring of a Mozart serenade. Wild, wide, precipitous, rough – and yet with a sylvan beauty and grandeur vastly appealing to a hard core of eminent artists who had been coming to the district to paint for over a century. Attractive, besides, to a growing horde of tourists. And here, in this setting, the forest acquisition officers had arrived to negotiate terms for securing land prior to the establishment of a national forest. Historic land in every sense, and imbued with many traditions.

These forest-trained men were aware of the high timber-growing potential of these valley slopes from certain historical data. For instance between 1754 and 1760, no less than £50,000 worth of oak had been felled and floated down the Conway from woods southeast of Betws-y-coed – and there were figures available of fellings, still uncompleted in 1920, from wartime clearance of timber by merchants.

They were aware, too, of the importance of landscape amenity in this famed locality for beauty, and also of economic considerations such as access, communication and transport. What, perhaps, they were not too confident about, was how well an extensive forest could be established on the ill-drained, exposed and complex topographical conditions prevailing on the upper levels beyond the valley ramparts – for much of this type of land would be included in the negotiations.

And so the transactions began . . . and this venture, this project, this concentrated planning of a vast state forest – a wedding between landscape and trees and the long honeymoon years of establishment – was got under way.

The initial survey laid emphasis on three factors:

(a) Favourable leasehold possession.

(b) The locality was an excellent one for a forest.

(c) There was ample scope for early extensions over surrounding moorland.

Features contained in the acquisition report covered a wide field. We will abstract a few to illustrate what form some of the recommendations took, and also to indicate the many complicated stages involved in such an enterprise.

The bulk of the land lay on the steep slopes on the west of the Conway valley and included a large tract of higher, plateau land. The Conway valley and tributary valleys (Lledr and Llugwy) were served with good roads and through the Conway and Lledr valleys ran the Llandudno-Ffestiniog branch of the then London and North-Western railway. The outlook for the transport of timber in the future was considered adequate, once it was got into the valley, though precipitous slopes in many instances would present considerable problems of extraction.

Dry masonry walls were in good condition and ought to help resolve the considerable fencing problems – it being light-heartedly assumed that little or no fencing would be necessary against sheep.

On the question of amenity it was pointed out that the whole location was a favourite tourist resort and there had been a clamorous outcry against the 1914–1918 fellings and wholesale clearance of timber. There was still a lot of timber to fell and this presumed further objections. Indeed, not all the timber had been sold and much of what remained was small oak and a few park-like units of hardwood of considerable visual attractiveness. Much attention, therefore, should be paid to the retention of the best oak scrub hardwood on small, uneconomic sites such as boulder scree and ledges.

Where possible also, some selected oak and ash could be incorporated into newly formed plantations, and hardwood transplants would be effective alongside prominent roadside locations. Certain conspicuous areas which had been felled (such as Pencraig Wood, overlooking the renowned Swallow Falls) ought to be replanted as early as possible, thus replenishing an otherwise barren slope and restoring, at the earliest opportunity, a tree-clad backcloth for these famous falls on the Llugwy.

The Forestry Commission, naturally, were keen to secure these plateau areas along with the devastated woods and those sites still in the process of being cleared, as this would swell the forest land total and make it more self-sheltering. Thousands of acres of moorland were involved and obviously this would be very difficult to afforest. The climax vegetation comprised associations of heather, heath, gorse, blue moor grass, deer grass, bilberry and bog myrtle, – a formidable league of competitors for small trees to become established in. Exposure was severe. Soils were acidic and shallow. The terrain was broken and rocky. Much drainage would be involved, with expensive operations. Except for one or two very minor council roads, communications over the uplands were

17

primitive. It was then – and remains – complicated and formidable afforestation territory.

It took courage, as well as responsibility, to negotiate for such land. The plateau lay between 500 and 1,000 feet above sea level. All it supported was a very thin sprinkling of sheep, grazed by smallholders, on the kinder vegetation types, and it was doubtful if the land would ever support more than one sheep to three acres. It was thus a most uneconomic area for the farmer.

CONDITION OF THE WOODS IN 1920

About 700 acres had been felled and a like area was due to come down before the land was handed over. About half the felled area was ready immediately for re-afforestation. Some 155 acres of young plantations, between the ages of four and ten years, could be taken over and there was much work to accomplish in these areas in the way of weeding, beating-up (replacement of failures) and draining. A large proportion of the felled woods had comprised pure coniferous crops but there were woods remaining to be felled which were composed of conifers mixed with oak, beech, sycamore and ash. Patches of pure European larch, Sitka spruce, Norway spruce and Scots pine also remained to be felled.

In the Carreg Gwalch and Aberllyn woods there was oak of excellent quality and splendid specimens of beech, larch, Scots pine, Weymouth pine, spruce and Silver fir. Much of the area, it was suggested, would be suitable for spruce, with Douglas fir confined to the lower, sheltered slopes. Owing to the steepness of many of these and the shaly character of the soil, there would be some risk of young trees being flattened by snow or blown by wind.

ALTERNATIVE PROSPECTS FOR LAND USE

If not re-afforested properly and efficiently the bulk of the felled areas would rapidly revert to wilderness and be of low economic value – indeed much of it could deteriorate due to the bare, steep slope-soils being washed away, with the predictable consequence of there being insufficient lodgement for grass cover as a stabilising factor.

One final word on amenity was included in the acquisition officers' initial report:

'Owing to the popularity of the district as a tourist centre a large proportion of the woods will be displayed to the full view of visitors. Careful planning of plantation layout and choice of species will be a capital advertisement of the Forestry Commission's intentions and activities – and this is a place where we must not fail, as scenic effects are jealously observed.' Thus, as long ago as 1920 the traditions of amenity were laid down, and complied with throughout the development of the forest. None but the most prejudiced could take exception to the grandeur of the scene today.

DETAILS OF THE LAND ACQUIRED

The initial survey was completed, and four separate blocks of land were offered to the Forestry Commission on long lease, comprising over 6,000 acres of valley slopes, moorland, smallholdings and pasture.

### BLOCK 1, WEST SLOPES OF CONWAY VALLEY

| Woods | acres | Smallholdings (continued) | acres |
|---|---|---|---|
| Main woodland block | 1757 | Clawdd Gwyn cottage and land | 6 |
| Coed Dolgarrog ⎫ | 131 | Llety cottage and land | 3 |
| Coed Gwydyr ⎭ | | Nant Uchaf cottage and land | 13 |
| Woods west of Llyn-y-parc | 12 | Nant Isaf land | 13 |
| Hafotty Cae'n-y-coed | 17 | Bwlch yr Haiarn cottage and land | 3 |
| Part Coed Craig, Glan Conway | 7 | Pen y Parc cottage and land | 4 |
| Smallholdings | | | |
| Penrallt Penucha'r Allt Cottage | ·3 | | |

Block 1 had a total of 1,966 acres and comprised a high percentage of derelict woodland, much of it on the very steep western slopes of the Conway Valley. Very little moorland was included here, but small areas in the Llugwy Valley spread this particular block from Dolgarrog in the north to points south-east and south-west of Betws-y-Coed. A few smallholdings (cottages and land) were incorporated.

### BLOCK 2, NORTH OF BETWS-Y-COED

| | acres | | acres |
|---|---|---|---|
| Mynydd Bwlch yr Haiarn sheepwalk | 211 | Pen yr Allt Uchaf ⎫ | |
| Bryn Fawnog cottage and land | 5 | Pen yr Allt Ganol ⎬ 153 | 153 |
| Sarnau (two cottages and ⎫ | | Tan y Castell ⎭ | |
| mountain grazing) ⎬ 183 | 183 | Coed Mawr Holding ⎫ | 137 |
| Fridd cottage ⎭ | | Coed Mawr Mountain ⎭ | 202 |
| Ty'n y Mynydd cottage and land | 15 | Pen yr Allt cottages | ·025 |
| Llidiart y Gwynt | 10 | Pen yr Allt Isaf | 135 |
| Haffoty Pencraig ⎫ | 59 | Aberllyn | 37 |
| Hafod yr Ewen ⎭ | | | |
| Penycraig holding | 105 | | |
| Ty'n llwyn (two cottages) | ·5 | | |
| Allt Isaf cottage and land | 16 | | |
| Diosgydd Isaf cottage and land | 28 | | |
| Diosgydd Uchaf holding | 154 | | |

Priority treatment was needed in Block 1, since most of the devastated woods lay in full view of the much-frequented Conway Valley environs, and there was an urgent need to restock the ground and secure the traditional 'tree scene' continuity with as little delay as possible.

In Block 2 the tree planters would be firmly entrenched on moorland plateau country with a total of 1,450 acres. Of the four blocks this one held the highest proportion of questionable plantable land. Practically the whole area was situated west and south-west of Llyn Parc and embodied rugged, bleak, broken terrain with much rock outcrop. Most of the holdings held little good pasture and required extensive repairs; the sheepwalks and mountain appeared inhospitable for the introduction of trees. All in all a courageous acquisition, though if suitable tenants were in occupation of the holdings, there was every possibility of a useful labour force, scattered strategically over an area of high fire risk.

### BLOCK 3, SOUTH-WEST OF BETWS-Y-COED

| LOCATION | AREA | | AREA |
|---|---|---|---|
| | *acres* | | *acres* |
| Cae Mawr holding | 154 | Part Pentre Ddu land | 8 |
| Craig Forys holding | 133 | Hafodlas holding | 95 |
| Hafotty Cae'n y Coed | 73 | Gartheryr holding | 125 |
| Part Cae'n y coed | 49 | Pen y Clogwyn cottage and land | 5 |
| Maesnewyddion | 131 | Rhiwgri holding | 69 |
| Wyddfyd | 72 | Part Tan yr Allt sheepwalk | 48 |
| Mynydd Cribau sheepwalk | 185 | Mynydd Bychan holding | 248 |
| Ty Mawr holding | 47 | Llanerch Elsi holding | 166 |
| Canol yr Allt cottage | ·19 | Cwmdreiniog holding | 157 |
| Pant yr Hyddod holding | 110 | Cwm Celyn holding | 176 |
| | | Part Trawsafon land | 4 |

This gave a total of 2,055 acres. However, in 1924 an area of 8·3 acres was submerged to provide a reservoir for Betws-y-coed, and this we now know as Llyn Elsi. This block consists of valley slopes and moorland south and south-west of Betws-y-coed and between the valleys of the Llugwy and Lledr. Visual amenity considerations would need to be kept much to the fore. Topographically, the plateau land here was somewhat more rounded in character, and less broken than in Block 2, though again there were problems of exposure, peaty soils, and difficult drainage areas to contend with. In general, the holdings had better pasture and meadow conditions, and contained a higher proportion of larger agricultural units than the other blocks.

Llyn Crafnant and Craig Wen.

Bryn Engan & Garth Llwyd holding        610 *acres*

An isolated area in the North-north-east foothills of Moel Siabod, immediately south of Capel Curig. Again, much of the location must be planned in visual amenity terms, there being a fine stand of natural oak as a representative ecological unit on the flank adjacent to the main road and village.

These four blocks entailed an acquisition of over 6,000 acres or nearly ten square miles. What an area for the formation of a large forest! To the west the fractured skyline of the highest mountain range in Wales, violet-hued of a summer evening, coldly detached and glittering under a winter frost. Closer, the broken configuration of the rugged foothills, embracing the clefts wherein the passes ran through to western Caernarvonshire. Then, within the future forest boundary, the heather-clad plateau moors with their dozen or so lakes set amid graphic scenery, the steep-sided beauty of the Llugwy and Lledr valleys, the waterfalls, streams and quiet retreats. One wonders what passed through the minds of these men sent here to negotiate this acquisition . . . what they felt as they gazed to the west and south and north over these extensive upland ranges? Certainly, first and foremost, the potential suitability of the land as a forest; but did they, in their mind's eye, visualise the scenes as we see them today, fifty years on? The serrated skyline of conifers . . . the range of colours and shades . . . the vast impact of the tree population on the windswept plateau . . . the huge contribution of raw material for industry?

Of the holdings in Block I – the first lease negotiated – six of the tenants were labourers and one a carter for the estate, and it was felt that these men would welcome the prospect of employment with the Forestry Commission. They all had limited experience of plantation work and could form the nucleus of the forest staff of the future.

The agricultural tenancies were yearly, running from 30th November, in accordance with local custom; cottage tenancies ran from 1st May. In actual fact, the Forestry Commission secured the mountain land on a 999-year lease at a very reasonable rental per acre per annum.

MARKETS AND ACCESSIBILITY

Generally remote from consuming centres, though rail and road arteries would fulfil transportation purposes. Up to 1914 all the timber that was felled went for estate purposes. With the advent of war in 1914 however, supplies were despatched all over the country and all the larger timber was converted to various forms of scantling.

All the area in Blocks 1, 2 and 3 were already let to the tenants as small upland grazing farms. There were over fifty holdings involved and of the total area rather more than 500 acres was enclosed land consisting of more or less improved pasture with a small proportion of arable land. The latter did not exceed 120 acres and the total percentage of enclosed land to the whole area would be about 13%; 87% comprising rough mountain grazing, the general density of grazing being in the region of 0·8 sheep per acre.

SUGGESTED TREE SPECIES

Spruce would occupy the largest proportion of land. Valley slopes would support Douglas fir, and Scots pine had an important role on the drier, upper sites. One-fifth of the complete area was assumed capable of producing larch of good size, and beech was proposed as a mixture on the lowest valley slopes and along roadsides.

FIRE RISK

Considered high on the moorland areas.

PROBABLE PRODUCTION AND ASSESSMENT OF QUALITY

There were few data or former experience to guide people, and future estimates were difficult to predict. But some measurements of trees – a Norway spruce at Garth Eryr had a top height of 122 feet and a volume of 298 cubic feet – provided reasonably accurate figures.

Assuming that the land was planted in the proportion 55% spruce, 20% larch, 20% pine and 5% Douglas fir, and presupposing a 78% production, the average final yield of all species worked out at 4,640 hoppus cubic feet an acre. In round figures, after allowing for thinning-out as the crops matured to an estimated age of 70 years, three tons of timber could be harvested each year from every acre of established forest.

The Gwydyr Estate reserved:

(a) All mines, minerals and ores, together with the rights of working and removing same.
(b) The mine buildings and premises on the existing workings.
(c) Water rights and easements.
(d) Chapel and school at Bwlch yr Haiarn.

Sporting, over the whole 6,000 acres, with the exception of

fishing, was included in the lease at a low rental as it had been adversely affected for several years due to the felling of woodland cover.

## GENERAL PROPOSALS FOR WORKING

It would be necessary to find a nursery site (or sites) and relate the size to an annual planting acreage programme. Assuming a planting programme of 400 acres per annum, roughly 700,000 plants would be required for this area and for replacing failures.

## ALLOCATION FOR FIRST FIVE YEARS, 1921–1926

| | |
|---|---|
| Smallholdings | 4,156 acres |
| Nursery | 25 acres |
| Woodlands and Plantation | 1,900 acres |

Smallholders should be disturbed as little as possible. Some were likely to give up their tenancies of their own accord, and holdings becoming vacant in this way should be taken in hand immediately and planted. The remainder were to give up part of their mountain land only a little at a time and several years' notice of this intention was to be given them. It was essential to try and plant up the felled woodland areas first.

## LABOUR

Only a small labour force was immediately available. But the lead mines in the vicinity were closing down and here there could be a pool of labour, which, if not adjusted to forestry work, was at least used to working in the conditions pertaining to the high moors and plateau country.

## DIVISION OF FOREST LAND

(1) *Acquired plantations from the estate.* These were growing poorly and would require a great deal of attention. (High Parc, Haffoty Cae'n y Coed, Clogwyn Gwlyb, Fuches-Las.)

(2) *Devastated woods.* Felled in the 1914–1918 war, and those areas still in process of being felled and cleared. These operations were likely to continue until 1926 or 1927. On steep-sided valley slopes for the most part and along the edge of the plateau land.

(3) *Moorland.* A fringe of thin soils, steep and craggy in character, with scree and peat hollows. Typical 'ffridd' land.

*Plate 4.* Troed-yr-Afon, where Lledr stream joins Conway River below Fairy Glen oakwoods.

*Plate 5.* Young trees of British Columbian Grand Fir, under light birch cover.

*Plate 6.* Forest road through ninety-foot tall Douglas firs, north of Miners Bridge. Aged forty-five years, these trees were raised from seed imported from Oregon.

*Plate* 7. River Llugwy, near Miners Bridge, Betws-y-Coed.

*Plate* 8. Hill pastures below Moel Siabod, Capel Curig.

*Plate 9.* The Llugwy Gorge courses past Swallow Falls east to Betws-y-Coed.

*Plate 10.* Swallow Falls Hotel. Looking south across Llugwy Valley from Craig-yr-Hafod.

(4) *Plateau country.* Complex, exposed, rugged moor with wide and variable vegetation associations:

Rushes – *Molinia* – mosses – *Vaccinium* (bilberry).
Heather – *Molinia* – *Vaccinium* – *Myrica* (bog myrtle).
Pure heather.
Heather *Erica* – *Molinia.*
Heather – gorse.
*Trichophorum* – *Erica* – *Molinia.*
*Nardus* – *Eriophorum* – *Juncus* – *Molinia.*

This was the most difficult of all areas to afforest.

## ROADS

Local authorities maintained various public roads traversing the different blocks. These were narrow, tortuous and often very steep. The only other rights of way – admitted to be actually dedicated to the public – were the Jubilee path from Betws-y-Coed to Clogwyn Cyrau and from Betws-y-coed to Elsi Lake. Other rights and easements existed to various smallholdings and the mines, but these followed existing tracks and rides and would not seriously impede on Forestry Commission operations. No common or manorial rights existed over any of the land.

### EXTRACT FROM THE SCHEDULE OF BUILDINGS

*(Indicating the type of property the Forestry Commission took over in 1920.)*

| Name of property | Description |
| --- | --- |
| Bryn Fawnog | 4-roomed cottage, stone built. Slated lean-to shed and a Dutch barn. |
| Ty'n y Mynydd | 5-roomed cottage, stone built and slated, with barn, cow-house and piggeries. |
| Pencraig | 8-roomed house and two-storied outbuildings, stable, barn, cowhouse and calfhouse, covered cart-shed. |
| Penrallt Isaf | 4-roomed cottage, bakehouse, dairy, cowhouse, stable, calfhouse, stone built and slated. |
| Hafod y Wern | 2-roomed cottage. |

These scattered properties, along with the remainder, formed small agricultural units throughout the area. The majority were located on the plateau land or on the upper levels of the valley slopes, and were obviously of potential value to the Forestry Commission in two ways. Firstly, they provided habitation for forest tenants, the population of which would increase as the forest expanded; secondly, they would maintain the continuity of maxi-

25

mum land use by concentrating on only the best land for improvement and preservation. An average of some 10 acres of such land was envisaged per holding.

And so 6,000 acres of land came into the hands of the Forestry Commission. It was the first instalment in the area. Later, other large leases were successfully negotiated – the Glyn area of 1,075 acres, part of the Penrhyn estate (5,759 acres), Bwlch (682 acres), Cwm Penanman (1,815 acres), Hafod Gwenllian (592 acres), Hendre, Crafnant (626 acres), Bennar (1,084 acres). Indeed acquisitions to the forest continue to this day, though many comprise detached areas often miles away from the main forest blocks.

But the Gwydyr acquisition was the initial one. Here, would be the birth of the project. Just what would the reaction be? How much criticism would be forthcoming? Could a large afforestation scheme on the difficult uplands be successful? Would an extensive coniferous forest area wed in with the landscape? There was a long tradition of popular tourist and artist attractions here – people were accustomed to a wooded backcloth to the Llugwy and Lledr valleys. These, however, had been mixed in character with an emphasis on natural hardwoods such as oak, ash and beech. Now, a vast area of fast growing conifers was planned for many of the valley slopes and all the hinterland of rough moor.

'Tread warily' was the Commission's dictum; consult and meet various local representative bodies and explain our plans. Secure their comments, and wherever possible, respect their opinions, assuming they were practicable and not merely adverse criticism for criticism's sake. Because, despite all the representation, a national forest was to be established – this was both a statutory obligation and a natural need. Here were thousands of acres of completely unproductive land. Forestry would be of great economic significance to the district, both by taking up the poor land and by expanding employment of local labour. The lead mines and the slate quarries were fast running down – what could better absorb the redundant workmen and provide employment for decades ahead?

The Road to Llyn Geirionydd.

## Chapter 3

# THE FIRST DECADE: GENESIS
## 1921–1930

"I often wish'd that I had clear
for life, six hundred pounds a year,
A handsome house to lodge a friend
A river at my garden's end,
A terrace walk, and half a rood
Of land, set out to plant a wood."

*Jonathan Swift.*

PLANTING BEGAN IN 1921 in a post-war period of re-adjustment, national self-appraisal, and uncertainty. Lloyd George headed a coalition government, and it was the commencement of a momentous decade throughout the world, including prolonged intervals of industrial depression.

At Gwydyr the forest became established. Its birth was not without difficulties – protracted ones – for its first five years were tended

27

by inexperienced supervisors and a small estate staff recruited from the available smallholdings. Apart from new areas to establish, there were scattered acreages of acquired woodlands to tend and the holdings to be maintained and improved. Teething troubles were inevitable in such a large and complex project as the initiation of a state forest.

Obstacles were magnified during the first five years because of:

(a) The lack of trained, experienced forest supervisors.

(b) A relatively small number of only partially-skilled workmen.

(c) The gradually accumulating arrears in maintenance work necessary, both for the acquired woodland areas and the newly established plantations.

(d) Sheep trespass.

(e) The widely scattered locations of annual planting programmes.

(f) Limited knowledge of technique by the estate labour force newly transferred to forestry.

This period was devoted to replanting those areas felled and cleared during the first world war. Nine hundred and nine acres were re-afforested in the first three years – an ambitious, bold undertaking under the circumstances, for adequate supervision was limited and the labour force largely unskilled. Inevitably, weeding and cleaning of plantations fell into arrears, and insufficient drainage was undertaken. Although the fringe of the plateau country was approached at High Parc and Tancastell, planting was confined to the steep-sided slopes in the Llugwy valley and the western side of the river Conway. The species used over most of the early-established areas comprised Douglas fir on the lower, sheltered ground, European larch on the intermediate slopes, Scots pine on the thin-soiled ridge tops and spruce on moist sites at all levels. Three belts of Corsican pine were tried on the Diosgydd bank, on a southerly aspect, and the only other species to break this pattern was Japanese larch, introduced in Coed Pencraig in 1923.

What is often overlooked, when we consider – perhaps with some doubt – whether these early selections of species were correct or not, was the factor of a rapidly changing plant environment. Right up to the time of enclosure for planting, intensive sheep grazing had been persistent for decades. This exerted a control on certain vegetation associations, and gorse and heather, in particular, were not easily detected as potential major plant communities on grassland with rock fairly close to the surface.

Immediately fences were erected, and sheep excluded, the gorse invasion was on, changing the complex of the habitat and engaging thousands of young trees in intensive competition. The intensity of this sudden conversion had not been anticipated and it meant expensive and prolonged weeding. Doubtless, had this factor been expected, a change of species would have been desirable on some sites, though the emergence of gorse was inevitable.

Oddly enough, gorse – particularly in the High Parc region – had contributed a great deal to horse feed. This area, sparsely stocked with timber, carried a constant gorse crop and this was cut by Gwydyr estate staff when still young and succulent, and carried down to a silo at Gwydyr Uchaf for conversion to silage. The estate used to treat the area on a selective gorse cycle, cutting so many acres this year, moving on to adjacent sites next year and returning perhaps in two or three years' time to the initial cutting zone. The Wynn family were ardent horse lovers and Lady Mary Wynn used to favour a particular bridle path which led up through the woods to Llanrychwyn and the church there.

IN 1923 the Technical Commissioner – a senior member of the Commission's staff – visited Gwydyr and emphasised that the work of developing the forest called for special attention. He made reference to sheep trespass and the nibbling and biting of trees – an increasing scourge – and enumerated the consequence of the damage: (a) Spruce on difficult ground conditions could perish or suffer reduced vitality, thus remaining indefinitely in a checked condition, (b) Larch tended to survive some sheep damage, though nibbled side shoots contributed to a spindly growth-form, (c) Many plants got pulled up when being chewed and were consequently loose in the ground.

Rabbits were a problem, too. A high population inhabited the rock-strewn slopes and 'ffridds' and on terrain of this nature fencing was exceptionally difficult and certainly not 100% effective. Systematic trapping seemed the only practicable answer.

1924 saw the systematic establishment of Forest Workers' Holdings incorporated into forest policy. It was designed that each holding should consist of enclosed agricultural or cultivatable land of approximately 10 to 15 acres, together with such additional grazing land as might be available. The holder was guaranteed not less than 150 days employment in the forest throughout the year. An economic rent was to be charged. The holdings were not intended to be self-supporting and the Forestry Commission desired to create one holding for every 200 acres of land afforested where practicable. A reconstruction programme was put into effect on these lines and Diosgydd Isaf was the first completed holding, being ready for occupation in the autumn of 1925.

It became necessary to form a small squad to accomplish these estate projects and the magnitude of the work should not be disparaged. Many of the holdings were in very bad condition; nearly all were in isolated spots reached only by cart tracks; trained labour was in short supply.

IN 1926, a relatively small planting programme of 98 acres was undertaken, and this year marked the first introduction of fully-trained supervisors. The suspension of a larger planting programme was due to the heavy backlog of replacing failed trees; there were failures of up to 55% in groups in 1923–24 areas. Gorse weeding had become a great problem; it could not be cut back too severely or the trees either got too drawn up and spindly or were bent by wind. On Diosgydd Bank hundreds of fir and larch had to be staked, and the gorse only cut back in a circle immediately around the trees to encourage adequate lateral growth.

Prior credence that stone walls were sufficient to keep sheep out of planted areas was now revoked, and for the first time 7 foot 6 inch wall stakes, with a double strand of barbed wire, were used.

Only Diosgydd nursery was retained after this year – former nurseries at Pen-y-Parc and Gwydyr Uchaf being gradually abandoned. As Diosgydd was on a fairly steep slope, seed sowing was discontinued and the nursery used for transplant production only. It was to give worthwhile results for over another twenty years.

The Dolgarrog Dam disaster occurred in the autumn of 1925, when the retaining wall of an upland dam was breached, and a huge volume of released water poured downwards through many houses at the northern end of Dolgarrog village in the lower Conway valley. Great boulders were torn out and swept down the steep ravine, and the debris may be seen to this day. Many lives were lost in the sudden, brief terror, and as soon as word was received of the disaster, many forestry men were despatched to the scene to help in clearing and rescue operations. The initial rumble of the catastrophe was heard in the Llugwy Valley, eight miles away.

This year saw the emergence of a new policy in the acquisition of land. This was, to restrict acquisitions, so far as possible, to land of low value for any other purpose, and after ascertaining the net revenue, to arrange a fair price upon that basis. Reconstruction of the derelict holdings continued throughout 1926. Penrallt Uchaf, Tancastell, Penrallt Isaf, Alltwen, Penrallt cottage and Ty'n Llwyn were all completed, and tenants moved in as soon as they became available. Labour problems arose over wages and conditions, but these were generally attributed to the non-tenant faction – part-time ex-miner employees from Llanrwst and Trefriw. Some of the mines were still partly operating and it was a common sight to observe miners walking across the hills to or from their work.

Supervisory staff were involved in an enormous ration of walking and cycling; there were no vehicles, and only footpaths and bridle paths to utilise. Across the plateau lands, up the rough, steep hillsides from Dolgarrog to the Lledr valley approaches, constituted the daily routine – a routine of considerable physical endurance. For it entailed plantation inspection and assessment, control of the estate staff, supervision of workmen, tenancy factors, fire patrol and liaison with adjacent landowners. The men who were in at the birth certainly knew every inch of the ground – who wouldn't after a daily 15–20 mile stint?

Contractors were still felling the remaining hardwoods in the Miner's Bridge, Aberllyn and Gwydyr Uchaf woods, and four and six-horse teams hauled out the produce, on waggons. Portable sawmills were in evidence; there was activity everywhere to get felling completed, so that forest gangs could begin the work of preparing the ground for replanting. Much of the best timber had been felled between 1914–18 and in the interval heavy coppice regrowth had invaded the areas. This, plus the lop-and-top left by the merchants, involved heavy cost to clear.

THE 1927 PLANTING PROGRAMME, though not large, was prolonged by very high commitments to replace failed trees. This problem of catching up on arrears, of replacing failures established four or five years previously, was an extremely vexatious one. More so, because of the scattered nature of the plantations and the very difficult ground conditions.

Planting equipment comprised the Schlich spade, the garden spade, the circular spade, dibble and axe mattock.

Scree and semi-scree presented planting problems. What little good-form natural hardwood that was surviving – oak, rowan, holly, birch, sycamore – was retained, since these were scattered and light crowned, but the absence of reasonable soil depth precluded a complete planting. To redress this, a framework carrier was made, capable of holding six cardboard containers filled with soil and with a transplant planted in each. The carrier was then carried up on to these scree sites by two men, and the individual containers lifted out and distributed among the scree at reasonable spacing. Douglas fir and European larch on the Aberllyn-Carreg Gwalch area were treated in this manner, yielding a 75% establishment figure, and stocking some 10 to 15 acres of otherwise doubtfully plantable land. A somewhat primitive method perhaps, but on such an area justified for the effort alone, when one considers that replacement of failures was not needed, and apart from some staking against windrock at a later date, these difficult sites were adequately re-afforested.

Fire danger was now increasing, through the establishment of plantations alongside the railway in the Lledr Valley, and the increase in hikers using the innumerable paths through the forest.

1927 WAS THE FIRST YEAR that Silver firs and Western hemlock were introduced on a moderate scale. Groups were established in the Miner's Bridge area, along with some Serbian spruce and a plot of Californian redwood. The site here was comparatively well-sheltered, with ample rich, deep soil, and had previously supported hardwood of excellent quality. Oak coppice of good form had to be cut away before re-afforestation could proceed.

Seven new bungalow-type forest workers' holdings were erected before the end of the year – two in Lledr Valley, four flanking the Glyn area and one at Pencraig. The design was a great step forward in amenity and location.

1928 WITNESSED A MUCH LARGER PLANTING PROGRAMME with extensions to land outside the initial Gwydyr acquisition – on to the Glyn and Gallt-y-foel. Previously all the planting was confined to the re-afforestation of felled woods. Now, for the first time afforestation of a large section of extensive sheep-grazed mountain started. This took place on the Glyn, an undulating, broken plateau, characterised by several north to south ridge formations and some picturesque lakes. This western portion of the north block has a character all its own. It is close to the main Snowdonia foothills, remote and lonely. It has been the scene of long and painstaking effort to achieve tree establishment on some of the forest's most difficult ground. The topography is unusual in its very clearly defined ridge and hollow formations. Some of the basins are of exceptionally deep peat, needing pre-planting drainage.

Before 1928, this sheep-grazed mountain was characterised by the following three main vegetation types: (a) *Calluna-Erica – Molinia*-mosses, (b) *Nardus-Myrica – Trichophorum-Juncus*, (c) *Vaccinium*-light bracken-fine grasses. The bracken was restricted to the drier slopes with a south and east aspect, and sometimes associated with *Vaccinium* or bilberry. Mosses occurred throughout.

Enclosure was completed and sheep grazing stopped. Within a few months, certainly by mid-summer 1928, gorse, in increasing vigour, began to appear. This expanded in area, thickened, and began indeed to become dominant. Areas, previously considered as requiring but light annual weeding, were by 1930 committed to a heavy gorse cutting programme. The transformation was remarkable and deceptive.

Consequently the Glyn, throughout its establishment (1928–32), and for many years after demanded increasing attention to draining and gorse control. It has proved to be one of the most difficult areas to afforest, even with the introduction of plough planting in later years. It has remained notorious for its checked groups, and intensity of drain maintenance demands.

Timber merchants were still active in the Aberllyn-Carreg Gwalch area. All the clearing-up work was done by forest labour and this continued to be expensive, as the lop-and-top had to be burned, the unmarketable poles felled, and dense clumps of blackthorn eliminated. Planting also began in Denbighshire, at Gallt-y-Foel.

IN LATE 1928 there arrived the first of the miners and their families from South Wales, under the Distressed Areas scheme. Several of them occupied the bungalow-type holdings and quickly adapted to their new environment and working conditions.

At this time assistance to farming tenants, in the provision of lime, seeds, etc., and help in ploughing, was sanctioned up to a total of £5 per holding. Many holders took advantage of this and steadily built up better soil and grass conditions; others ignored both assistance and their holding obligations.

Of the lead mines, only Pool and Cyffty were operating intermittently and they were being run down. Maintenance work on the main levels seemed the prime concern – there was little extraction of ore. Pandora and Parc spluttered and ceased, and silence brooded over the huddle of buildings and the lonely pit-gear.

1929 WAS REALLY THE FIRST year when fires became prominent. The risk had, of course, always been recognised but until this year control measures, particularly on the dangerous Betws-y-coed to Gethin Viaduct stretch of the railway line, had confined outbreaks to small acreages here and there.

There were 17 fires between February 22nd and 30th May (including three on 8th March), and 89 acres were burned mostly on areas planted in 1925 and all in the Lledr Valley approaches. This, despite continued patrolling of the line after each train had passed. During dry intervals the fire risk was always high and the close proximity of the young plantations to the railway line, the steepness of the gradient (with the consequent stoking of the engine fire and the emergence of myriads of sparks) and the inflammable nature of vegetation within the plantation, combined to make life hectic and hot for the patrolmen. There were alarums and counter-alarums, smoke wisps here, smoke spirals there. And the blaze would creep and curl, and then sweep up the boulder-strewn slopes and into the plantations, perspiring patrolmen in pursuit, beating

33

Machno Bridge, below Penmachno.

at the flanks with their birch brooms, barking shins and arms on the heather and gorse-clad rocks. It was no fun. And in each succeeding year as the plantations gradually extended right up the Lledr Valley the patrol area increased and the risk area lengthened. Burned areas were replanted, then burnt again. Railway fires became a nightmare and fire reports thickened in the files.

It was suggested in 1929 that counter-firing in such a situation could perhaps prejudice any subsequent claim against a railway company for damages arising out of a fire they had occasioned. But this was refuted, in that counter-firing (whenever practicable) was completely justified and necessary, and therefore there could be no prejudice against claims. But conditions had to be just right for effective, safe counter-firing. In the confines of a narrow valley, and on broken gorse and heather-clad hillside, counter-firing measures could only be limited in application. Only the progressive experience and dedication of the patrolmen helped contain the outbreaks.

The small group of ex-miners alluded to earlier were quick to settle down. Three of them prepared the ground and undertook their first planting in March 1929 in the area Miner's Bridge – Pool mine (between the river Llugwy and the main Holyhead road). The species was Japanese larch and the result a thoroughly good take. (Later, much later, a son of one of these men was to prune these same trees and another son to undertake the first thinning out. Thus, one family had a connection with this particular plantation spanning some twenty years – a pleasing example of continuity.)

The plateau country was now invaded with the establishment of pine, larch and spruce on the exposed Pandora block. This was one of the most unfavourable locations in the forest, thin-soiled, rocky, inhospitable, bleak. When it came to planting time a severe frost held up operations for weeks in other parts of the forest. This was accompanied by a thoroughly cold east wind which persisted throughout February. Yet on Pandora, with its dense mat of heather, the peat ground remained free from iron-clad frost effects, and planting was undertaken in bitterly cold conditions with a surprisingly low mortality rate. Scots pine, in particular, established themselves excellently.

On the Glyn, the first turf planting in Gwydyr was accomplished with Norway spruce near Ty'n-y-mynydd lake. This was on irregular wet patches around the south-west lake edge. A visiting forest officer proposed trials of Sitka and Norway spruce and Japanese larch seedlings on turves, and a year later an area was so treated just north of Llyn Goddion-duon. Overall planting reached the record figure of 628 acres.

A reminder of the Commission's amenity obligations emphasised that the lay-out of all plantations should include consideration of visual effects. Endeavours were to be made to meet all reasonable requirements of interested local bodies.

1930 WAS A YEAR OF NATIONAL ECONOMIC CRISIS and severe economy measures were applied throughout the country. Forestry did not escape. Maintenance work on holdings was curtailed; plantation upkeep – particularly draining and fencing – suffered. Cleaning of tree crops on many areas was eliminated from the programme, though increasing regrowth of coppice on many of the valley slopes was becoming a serious factor in plantation development. Piece-work rates were inevitably affected – for example, a planting rate was cut from 14/– to 12/– per 1,000 trees put in.

Areas planted in 1930 stretched from Penmachno (Llechwedd-hafod) in the south to Coed-y-wern (Trefriw) in the north. Ground conditions for planting were very much kinder in the Machno valley area, but Gwydyr still had vast acreages of really difficult, thin-soiled plateau country to be dealt with.

On the eastern fringe of the Glyn, plots of Western hemlock, Grand fir and Western red cedar were planted on rocky terrain supporting a few old oak standards. Along the Nant Bwlch y Haiarn road a small area was given over to Noble fir and Californian redwood.

The gradual improvement to holdings and attached land had been a significant factor in stabilising a somewhat refractory labour force, though it was not always possible to get the better, semi-skilled workman and his family to occupy a remote upland holding. Slowly and perceptibly, however, the training of the better workmen was accelerating, and a spirit of 'forest consciousness' was being instilled. Many were now good nurserymen and had experience of planting, fencing and draining. The small estate staff had contributed much to getting holdings in good shape for occupation.

## THE FIRST DECADE – CONCLUSIONS

The foundations had been established reasonably well despite many handicaps. Two thousand, nine hundred and sixty-two acres had been planted, and though much of this acreage included re-afforestation of felled woodland, the exposed upland terrain to the north of the river Llugwy was now clothed with nearly 1,000 acres of conifer.

The pattern had not materially altered throughout. Douglas fir remained first choice on the lower, sheltered slopes in the valleys of the Llugwy, Conway and Lledr. This type of ground was very boulder-strewn and terraced by rock outcrops, though soil depth was generally good and there was adequate natural drainage. On the upper slopes and along the fringes of the plateau country European larch was extensively used until 1927, though after this the Japanese variety acquired favour. Many European larch areas were dogged with intense gorse and coppice competition and growth-rate was slow. It was felt that Japanese larch would adapt quicker and would form canopy earlier due to a faster rate of growth. Sitka and Norway spruce had been used extensively on all moister zones at all elevations. Scots pine was confined to the heather knolls and the thin-soiled summits of crags and ridges.

Lodgepole pine emerged as a potentially successful species for exposed heather sites after 1928, and was increasingly used to beat-up checked spruce and Scots pine areas on the poorest peats and the direr gorse/*Erica*/*Molinia* knolls. It promised to show tolerance of extremely poor soils, exposure and drought. Corsican pine had only been used on a limited scale – in 1921, 1923 and 1926. The first time was on Diosgydd bank (a south aspect), the second at Coed-y-wern (an east aspect), and thirdly on a north-north-east aspect in the Lledr Valley. Some doubt as to its suitability on high elevations had been expressed, though its growth on all these sites throughout the decade had been good. Of the minor species, the Silver firs in Miner's Bridge were growing rapidly, and Western hemlock on the same site and up on the eastern fringe of the Glyn looked promising. Poplar growth in Waterloo Spinney had been outstandingly good.

FIRE

Inevitably, fire risk was increasing. The railway, the increase in hikers, steam waggons on the roads, and the indiscriminate burning of hill grasses by adjoining farmers, were all contributory factors to the need for ever-mounting vigilance. The scattered nature of the young plantations, not many of which were yet at the thicket stage, and the inflammable nature of vegetation everywhere, added to the potential hazard. The railway patrol systems were here to stay, and it was becoming necessary to post patrols at week-ends and holiday periods, during the spring and summer months, in those areas bisected by frequently-used public footpaths.

CLEANING AND WEEDING PLANTATIONS

Coppice had been widespread in many of the older plantations, particularly on old woodland sites. Gorse had become a real problem with the exclusion of sheep and had increased its range. Heather and bracken areas were weeded more economically.

## LABOUR

We couldn't expect first rate labour. In the first place there was no forest tradition to live up to; secondly, the early-years labour force was untrained, many of them ex-lead miners who didn't remain long; thirdly, it took time to accommodate the better-class men in holdings and train them, and in the fourth place the long walking distances between plantations and holdings deterred many. The few who were taken over from the Gwydyr estate staff became the backbone. All were accommodated in holdings by 1928; all were reasonably versatile. To these could be added a dozen or so other tenants, and youths who were taken on straight from school. By 1930, association with the growing forest had bred a certain 'forest consciousness' in most of them, and the first generation of 'Gwydyrites' had become established.

## NURSERY

Diosgydd, despite its rather steep slope, had yielded consistent results throughout the decade. Its sheltered, south-facing aspect was conducive to maximum sun and light influences and the soil was friable. As a transplant nursery – seed sowing was discontinued after 1926 – it fulfilled its purpose admirably, and a useful nursery staff had been recruited and trained.

## SUPERVISION

As the workers were silviculturally unskilled for the first half of the decade, this threw much responsibility on to supervisors in matters such as draining, plant replacement, weeding and cleaning. Push-bikes were the only means of transport and paydays involved a twenty – and quite often a thirty – mile journey. Inspections and daily routines averaged fifteen miles of walking a day between plantations, over rough, steep terrain. Despite these 'pioneer handicaps' the staff gained in local stature year by year, and a very good liaison was progressively built up with local authorities, farmers and residents.

## THE FOREST IMPACT

There will always be critics, and they were expostulative in the 20's as they are today. But by 1930, the really vitriolic critics could be counted on the fingers of one hand. The gradual building of the forest had intruded on the scene slowly; the transition did not convert a large area of land in any one year; close to the villages there was an unemotional acceptance of newly-established woods, and a very vociferous acceptance by local tradesmen, of the increase in spending capacity due to the Commission's presence. Local hauliers and ironmongers benefited too; the new forest community spent their money at the fairs and markets and the public houses. Artists, visitors and hikers acclaimed many aspects and denounced but few. The Forestry Commission was not alienated or maligned; indeed their external image received well-merited praise. Early days? Perhaps so; but at least the forest had come, it was seen, and by the vast majority, it was respected.

Lledr Valley, with Moel Siabod.

## Chapter 4

# THE SECOND DECADE: EXPANSION

## 1931–1940

> "If thou art worn and hard beset
> With sorrows, that thou would'st forget,
> If thou would'st read a lesson that will keep
> Thy heart from fainting and thy soul from sleep,
> Go to the woods and hills! No tears
> Dim the sweet look that nature wears."
>
> Sunrise on the Hills. *H. W. Longfellow.*

The Forestry Commission, established directly after World War I, completed its second decade in the initial throes of another.

The 30's were years of expansion, of enlargement over and into three separate valleys and across the hills between them. It was this

40

Plate *11*. The Holyhead road, A5, sweeps down the Llugwy Valley.

Plate *12*. Picnic site below Arboretum on Holyhead road near Swallow Falls.

*Plate* 13. On uplands north of Ugly House lie Llyn Bodgynydd Bach and beyond it larger Llyn Bodgynydd, haunts of water fowl. Moel Siabod rises south-west beyond unseen Llugwy Vale.

*Plate* 14. Llyn Elsi, reservoir on bleak heights south of the town which supplies Betws-y-Coed with water. Looking east towards hidden Lledr Valley and Tan-y-Clogwyn ridge.

decade that began the real forest impact upon the district. As the forest grew so the staff grew and the number of workers became stable; their spending capacity was reflected in the local villages. 'Working for the forestry' furnished a vote of confidence and not provocative rebuke; 'forestry people' now brought forth smiles to the shopkeeper's lips, rather than the earlier expressions of suspicion. The forest, and its people, had become a part of the scene, and their increasing contribution to economic and social wellbeing was now felt.

Forest workers' wives would ask each other, when they met in the shops or streets, where their husbands were working and what they were doing. 'Transplanting', 'Weeding', 'Cutting coppice' – these terms became incorporated into the language of the district. They were banded about in public bars and in the discreet seclusion of a snug; murmured among groups as they left the chapel precincts; voiced at local football matches and village sports and amidst the clamour of weekly markets. An outsider would have been forgiven for not caring to define them. It reminded one of Dr. Johnson, who while compiling his dictionary, defined 'postern' as the 'knee of a horse'. Asked by a lady how he came to do this, he replied with admirable frankness, 'Ignorance, madam, pure ignorance'.

The significant thing was that forestry, much of its terminology, and certainly all that it implied, was now very firmly acknowledged.

THE YEAR 1931 contained a large planting programme in widespread locations. Much afforestation was now progressing on the plateau land west of Llyn y Parc – Coedmawr, Pandora, the Glyn, and Diosgydd Uchaf. Further extensions on the Glyn acquisition were accomplished this year, and some ten acres of two-year old Sitka spruce seedlings were tried on turves, at $4\frac{1}{2}$ feet between rows and 3 feet between trees. Japanese larch seedlings were used on a part of Diosgydd mountain. Once again there was a critical shortage of good-sized plants of the correct species – larch was substituted for spruce on both the Glyn and on Diosgydd.

Complex areas, involving difficult drainage and turfing operations, were encountered on Pandora, north of Penrallt Ganol and on Diosgydd mountain. Between Diosgydd Uchaf and Hafod-yr-ewen there were many stretches of dense bog-myrtle, and turves were exceptionally difficult to cut; hundreds had to be carried over long distances.

Down in Waterloo Spinney some cleaning of the poplar area (planted in 1926) was undertaken, and a selective thinning to increase the quality and value of the better hardwoods was accomplished.

41

In a review of the planting programme for 1933, the decision was taken to reduce Gwydyr's figure from 500 acres to 400-odd, to help reduce the backlog of treating 'checked' plantations.

The first oak to be planted in the forest was at Penmachno (Coed y Plas). It was planted pure in one block and adjacent to it a single row mixture of oak and European larch was established.

Replanting of areas lost as the result of railway fires in 1930 and early 1931 was undertaken with Douglas fir on the characteristic boulder-clad lower slopes of the Lledr valley.

THE YEAR 1932 saw completion of afforestation on the Glyn acquisition, over 1,000 acres on the western flank of the forest. This former sheepwalk was let as a rough shoot, and fishing on the main lake – Goddion-duon – always provided some reward for one's efforts. It was too remote for a large concentration of visitors during the summer season, but the fire risk was high due to the burning of gorse and heather on adjacent ground to the west.

Under the Agricultural Wages (Regulation) Act of 1924:

(1) Employment in forestry shall be deemed to mean employment in connection with preparation of ground, planting and maintaining forest areas and nursery work in connection therewith.

(2) The wages payable for the employment of male workers shall not be less than wages at the following minimum rates:

21 years of age and over      35/– per 50-hour week
21   ,, ,, ,,   ,,   under 21   32/– ,,   ,,   ,,   ,,
15   ,, ,, ,,   ,,     ,,   16   20/– ,,   ,,   ,,   ,,

These were the day-rates applicable in 1932. Workmen travelled from their holdings to their place of work across the plateau land, and soon innumerable 'holder's footpaths' linked up the scattered sections of young forest. Short-cuts and detours can still be seen to this day, though vegetation clothes all but the most worn sections. There was a sharp cut in piecework figures due to national economy measures. Turf planting was reduced to 8/4 per 1,000 trees, that is, ten trees planted for one penny! Turf planting had now become standard practice on all the difficult wet areas, and apart from Coed Creigiau and Diosgydd Isaf, the bulk of the 526 acres planted was on turves. At Bwlch (Dolwyddelan) men travelled from Gwibernant to drain and turf-plant the area, and to save the long, arduous walk each day, some took three or four days' provisions with them and slept overnight in a barn located in the centre of the area (Beudy Brynbugelyn, meaning 'the bothy of the shepherds' hill'). The Bwlch was a severe fire danger region due to the indiscriminate burning of heather and gorse on adjoining land, by farmers.

On Wyddfyd, much inferior hardwood growing on precipitous rock outcrops was retained and conifers planted through it; while at Coed Creigiau the preparation of ground work involved cutting of heavy coppice and dense bramble at high cost.

Certain plantations were now developing well. High Parc (P 21 (i.e. planted in 1921), 22, 24), Diosgydd (P 21), Miner's Bridge (P 27), Coed y Wern (P 27) and Cae'n-y-Coed (P 28) were particularly uniform. Areas such as Glyn (P 28, 29), Ffrith Sian (P 27) and Pandora (P 29) still required considerable attention, but the plateau country afforestation was gradually proving successful – and despite difficulties over good-sized plants, lack of sufficient trees of correct species, and much maintenance work – this barren, inhospitable, unproductive terrain was taking on a new aspect.

IN 1933 came a sudden, unexpected decision. The planting programme – modified in the 1931 deliberations – was abruptly increased. Everything had to be hurried and there were only two animated weeks of planting time left. Yet it proved a fairly successful planting 'take' – and despite a long summer drought – growth was well above average. Bracken weeding was delayed until late summer due to the hot, dry weather and this contributed to the high survival rate.

Hafodgwenllian, hitherto an extensive sheepwalk of nearly 600 acres, proved a difficult area to drain effectively, owing to the configuration of the ground. Much deepening of main drains had to be done after the area was planted.

On the Bwlch (Dolwyddelan) the main species was spruce; on Alltwen and the Cwm Celyn-Cwm Dreiniog complex, Japanese larch, Sitka spruce and Scots pine. On this latter area the planting was pushed steadily up towards Elsi Lake where much of the ground was very poor, having a vegetation of *Erica cinerea*, *Calluna*, *Ulex*, *Molinia*, *Trichophorum* and *Nardus* grass.

Choice of species altered little. There was a suggestion that more Scots pine could be used on the uplands – on better sites – despite criticism of its susceptibility to high rainfall and snowbreak. In the early years Scots pine had been planted on many poor sites and condemned for its weak response and poor form. Lodgepole pine was emerging as a good tree for use in beating-up checked Scots pine areas on very exposed sites, and for planting on the dry heather knolls on all aspects.

Diosgydd Nursery had a full lining-out programme. It is of interest to record here the standard price for nursery stock in 1933. (Per 1,000 plants, free on rail to consignee's station – including packing, or direct from home nursery to forest.)

43

D*

| Age of tree: | 1 yr | 2 yr or older | 1 yr + 1 yr | 2 yr + 1 yr | 2 yr + 2 yr |
|---|---|---|---|---|---|
| | s. d. | s. d. | s. d. | s. d. | s. d. |
| Scots Pine | 4 0 | 6 0 | 19 0 | 24 6 | 33 6 |
| Japanese & European Larch | 5 0 | 10 0 | 25 6 | 35 6 | 43 6 |
| Norway Spruce | 2 6 | 4 0 | 11 0 | 16 6 | 22 6 |
| Sitka Spruce | 3 6 | 6 0 | 15 6 | 24 6 | 31 6 |
| Douglas Fir ⎫ Silver Fir ⎬ Red cedar, Cypress ⎭ | 9 6 | 13 0 | 28 6 | 38 6 | 44 6 |
| Oak | 11 0 | 14 0 | 43 6 | 38 6 | 53 6 |
| Ash & Sycamore | 6 0 | 8 6 | 23 6 | 33 6 | 38 6 |

The forest annual report drew particular attention to supervisory staff. The widespread nature of the forest, it emphasised, involved the head forester and foresters in walking and cycling distances of between forty and fifty miles every pay-day and up to twenty miles on any other day. This excluded the extra journeys made to investigate fires, etc., and a strong plea was urged to secure mechanical transport to facilitate communication and to help reduce the physical stress, particularly in inclement weather.

Forest workers' holdings were now nearly all filled and the tenants were employed practically full time.

The hare and rabbit population, despite full-time trapping, was increasing. The mountain hare had been observed on Ochre Fawr (Glyn) and at Pandora.

Fire considerations and responsibilities were now becoming onerous. The Lledr valley railway was a permanent alarm centre; the steeply-inclined track, low-powered engines and the increased stoking required, all contributed to risk. But the main-road danger was intensifying, both from steam lorries and wagons (many of them hauling slate from the Penmachno and Capel Curig quarries), and the increased emergence of the motor car and charabanc, from which the flipped unextinguished match and cigarette-end spelt immediate danger when conditions were dry. Furthermore, hikers were numerous on public footpaths, and tended to wander about indiscriminately, amidst, for the most part, plantations in the thicket stage and thus at their most vulnerable. Patrolmen were out in the Lledr valley, Diosgydd-Miner's Bridge, Parc Lake and Elsi Lake areas at all dry week-ends and over public holidays.

LAND PLANTED IN 1934 TOTALLED 487 acres. Most of it was on Hafodgwenllian, Tyddyn-du and the northern and western flanks of Mynydd Deulyn, between Lakes Geirionydd and Crafnant.

On Mynydd Deulyn, Japanese larch and Scots pine were established very well on broken, rocky ground up to 1,100 feet. Here, fencing difficulties arose owing to rock and the steepness of several ledge and outcrop pitches, and behind Glan Geirionydd House ropes were tied round the fencing team as a safety measure on two precipitous slopes dropping sheer to scree and boulder.

In five- to six-year old plantations (Coed-y-celyn, Aberllyn, Lledr valley, Hafna) coppice growth was increasing. On these old hardwood areas this was an inevitable process as re-growth could develop freely in competition with the young conifers. Some of the better-formed coppice growth was accepted on the rockier, drier sites where conifer stocking was thinly distributed.

The first thinning of some of the acquired estate plantations was undertaken in this year, thirty-eight acres of European larch on High Parc and Clogwyn Gwlyb. From the felling of oak overwood, 10,000 cleft stakes were made. Much of this conversion was done in snowy or hard-frost conditions and was a very acceptable and economic occupation when other work had to be suspended. The workmen became proficient too, and set-to with enthusiasm – it was the appropriate work for warming chilled limbs and setting an otherwise dispirited body to rights.

THE HIGH PLANTING RATE CONTINUED THROUGH 1935, when hinge-turf planting was introduced this year, at Ty'n-y-Cwm, on all the steeper ground, and 2+2 transplants provided good results. North American white spruce, *Picea glauca*, was planted there for the first time.

Of historical significance, this year witnessed the first establishment of plantations in the Gwibernant area – around Ty Mawr – birthplace of Bishop Morgan, the translator of the Bible into Welsh.

Fires showed a sharp decline in number and there were but two or three incidents involving small areas of plantation. This could be attributed to an increase in vigilance and efficiency rather than a more 'forest conscious' response from the public. Two key factors had played their part: (a) With the approval of their Headquarters, Automobile Association patrols now liaised very closely with forest staff. They were issued with maps, house locations of forest staff, telephone numbers, etc. It became a very efficient and rapid means of communication and covered the whole forest with the exception of the more westerly plantations on the uplands. (b) Forest patrol routines had become more competent and confident. In the event of a fire outbreak, and to obtain maximum assistance as soon as possible, forest patrols were issued with a supply of printed cards, which they handed to the first motorist they could stop. Motorists,

River Llugwy, oakwoods, and Moel Siabod, above Betws-y-Coed.

it was realised, might have been dubious about stopping on request, when confronted by an agitated, flush-faced, arm-waving patrolman, and to allay their suspicions, these notices were printed on thin fabric in large red letters, with the words: 'FOREST FIRE – PLEASE STOP'. In less bold lettering were a list of addresses and telephone numbers, and the patrolman would ask the motorist to call in at one of the addresses to report the warning or alternatively telephone a number. This was a large step in the right direction, and it involved delegating some responsibility to members of the public, who responded admirably when required.

Survival-rate assessments, undertaken during the summer, indicated that turf planting done in late January, throughout February and early March, returned the best results. There was increased success and efficiency with hinge and turf planting.

A labour training camp (later the Gwydyr Forest Training School), alongside the A.5 below Glyn farm, was now being built to house and train the unemployed. It was considered desirable that, ultimately, these men might participate in various forestry operations, such as road making, screefing vegetation from firelines, etc. As a prelude to this some surveying of a road line was done on the Glyn.

IN 1936 the first thinning of actual Forestry Commission plantations (as opposed to acquired areas) was undertaken. An area of 23 acres of European larch, planted in 1922, was thinned in High Parc. Sixty score rails were sold to local farmers and between 10–11,000 stakes were made, mostly split oak, but containing some larch from the thinnings.

It is significant to record that as Gwydyr's acreage expanded, and large areas of unproductive and inhospitable terrain was afforested the value of manufactured wood imported into the United Kingdom during 1936 was nearly £7,500,000 – comprising furniture, building woodwork, plywood, etc., – and the quantity of unmanufactured timber was 12,013,300 loads, valued at £43,569,000. Over £51,000,000 of imports in twelve months! A truly staggering sum – and only for this one indispensable and most versatile of material. These figures brought home the progressive future worth of the Forestry Commission's efforts and activities.

This year saw an increase in wages. Under the Agricultural Wages (Regulation) Act 1924, from April 19th 1936, the following minimum wages became payable for the employment of male workers.

21 years old and over    36/– per 50-hour week.
20 and under 21          33/– ,,  ,,   ,,   ,,
19  ,,    ,,    20        30/6 ,,  ,,   ,,   ,,

47

18 and under 19      28/– per 50-hour week
17  ,,    ,,   18     26/–  ,,   ,,   ,,   ,,

In January and early February, frost and snow held up work for six weeks. June and July were characterised by many thunderstorms and frequent outbreaks of torrential local rain. The autumn was exceptionally wet.

Produce sales were small. Fifty-three and a half score larch poles were sold to local farmers and 32 score to Musgraves of Chester. The Aluminium Corporation at Dolgarrog purchased 55 cubic feet of Douglas fir.

On Friday, February 14th, two fires swept into the Bwlch (Dolwyddelan), and 62 acres were lost. It was at one of these fires that a neighbouring farmer, setting out on horseback across the hill slopes to raise the alarm, was overtaken by the speed of the blaze and had to plunge to the flank to escape the sweep of flame. The fire was contained to 62 acres solely by dint of herculean efforts by a band of forest workers and two foresters, who fought the most rapidly burning fire experienced up to that time, and on the worst possible vegetation type: *Molinia*, heather and young four-year old spruce and pine plantation.

There were countless alarms along the railway line during spring – 20 fire reports being submitted for only the period 18th February to 10th March. A large fire swept across Gartheryr and Hafodlas in April, and workmen fought the blaze throughout the night. It did not penetrate any of the surrounding plantations.

THE YEAR 1937 brought a reduction in the planting programme – 331 acres – in accordance with the need expressed in earlier annual reports for an opportunity to be created to catch up on maintenance work. This year the Forestry Commission agreed to make the whole of Gwydyr forest into a National Forest Park.

Extensive areas were afforested at Hendre Crafnant on steep, rocky hillsides with many terraces, and at Penmachno (Henrhiw Isaf and Glasgwm valley). On the Bwlch (Dolwyddelan) part re-planting of the area burnt in February 1936 was accomplished, and the Wyddfyd plantations were extended into broken, high mountain land.

An unprecedented period of fire danger lasted through much of the exceptionally dry summer, though no serious outbreaks occurred. On 3rd May there were three fires, all of which were controlled before they invaded planted areas. In June, one relatively small fire occurred in an isolated, unplanted site containing gorse and heather, in the centre of hundreds of acres of plantation in the thicket stage. This fire required digging out – so deep and dry was the peat hereabouts – and operations continued for seven days, at a cost of over £80. There was no damage to plantations.

During the night of 27th-28th February 1937, twelve to eighteen inches of snow fell on all inland areas, accompanied by a northerly gale of great ferocity. (100 m.p.h. wind velocity was reported at Holyhead.) Locally, within the forest, this storm resulted in:

(a) 40-year old Norway spruce behind St. Mary's Church, Betws-y-coed, were almost all blown down or injured. These trees averaged 110 feet in height.

(b) Group blowing of trees in Douglas fir locations. (Planted in 1921, 22 and 25.) Size of group varied between ½ acre to 3–4 acres.

(c) Falling or loosening of individual trees or small groups. This necessitated much staking over an extensive area.

(d) Breaking and bending of terminal shoots. Douglas fir tended to straighten up, but Sitka spruce did not.

This snow storm was an unusual clinging type.

On the Glyn area, vertical sections were plotted on the first road alignment behind Glyn farm.

1938 WAS A DISASTROUS YEAR FOR FIRES, distinguished by the huge Parc fire of 11th/12th May, when 411 acres of plantation were lost. Much of this comprised thriving Norway spruce of P.21, 22, 23, 24 and 29 establishment; the remainder were areas in partial check on very rough ground.

Two other conflagrations accounted for 86 acres between them. At Tyddyn-du (Penmachno) 46 acres of Sitka and Norway spruce, planted in 1934, were lost. Here, a strong south-east wind fanned the blaze at an alarming rate and 30 acres were lost in 15 minutes. The burning vegetation – *Molinia* mostly – was carried for over 400 yards.

On the 30th of April, 40 acres were lost on Pandora. The fire started at 2 p.m. and was finally extinguished at 7 a.m. the following day. It spread into deep peat pockets and had to be dug out. Squads from the labour camp worked in relays all through the hours of darkness, assisting the forest staff. This was exceptionally difficult terrain to fire-fight over, being characterised by ridges, hollows and irregular rock outcrops, and the actual fire-front was indeterminate – creeping among rocks, down slopes, and burning for hours in the deep peat zones.

A measure of the fire risk, during the year, can be ascertained when nearly a three-and-a-half month drought was experienced from early February to mid-May – a period unbroken by any appreciable amount of rain. On the 18th April four fires were combated in the day; on the 3rd May it was five fires. There were 28

49

outbreaks on the railway line, though none caused damage to plantations. Forest staff endured a period of great trial and strain. The losses experienced, high as they were, would have been greater but for their tenacity and vigilance.

On the constructive side, 208 acres were planted, the bulk of the programme being at Crafnant and at Tanaeldroch, in the Lledr valley. On the latter area there were high amenity considerations and much beech was used. Hybrid larch made its introduction here, and Western hemlock and Western red cedar were also planted. Scrub-clad rock was left in its natural state, and groups of oak and other hardwoods were retained and underplanted with beech.

A swelling population of visitors were arriving throughout the summer. This influx reached peak periods when the 'Wakes' weeks holidays were in force – when each Lancashire cotton town closed down its mills in turn and the eager, good-hearted Lancastrians took to the holiday resorts along the North Wales coast, arriving by coach and excursion train, and making day visits to Betws-y-coed, the Swallow Falls, and other beauty spots in the district.

The Chairman of the Forestry Commission made a visit this year, and emphasised that Norway spruce should be still further restricted on the upland plateau and kept off all pure heather ground, with the exception of the better grass/bracken/heather types. In May, Colonel Ropner, M.P., a Forestry Commissioner, paid a visit to consider the proposals of the National Forest Park Committee.

The cleaning of plantations was now accelerating. Three hundred and ninety-three acres of coppice-cutting were completed, including Maesnewyddion, much of the Aberllyn area, Frith-Sian, Craig Glan Conway, Mynydd Bychan and Coed-y-Wern – all pre-1931 areas. The effect of coppice competition was seen to be emphasised in Douglas fir and Pine areas, particularly those not completely treated as the result of the 1930 financial restriction instruction, limiting expense on cleaning.

There was a maximum labour force of 95 in July and a minimum of 83 in December. Inspection for *Adelges* insects on Douglas fir showed that the incidence was much less than in 1937. It was negligible on Diosgydd and Maesnewyddion – the two oldest of large fir area plantings.

The total of vermin killed included 867 rabbits, 14 hares and eight foxes.

For the first time more than 100 acres of plantations were thinned in one year.

Experience had now been gained in setting equitable, economic piece-work rates, and costings had become more stable. Nevertheless, owing to the abruptly changing contrast in ground conditions over relatively short distances, the varying densities of coppice, gorse, heather and bracken on many sites and the extremely rough terrain over which miles of fences had to be erected and maintained, there were certain fluctuations in the price-range of maintenance work operations. In 1938, these prices applied to the following:

Cleaning — Between 15/– and 30/– per acre.
Draining upkeep — ,, 1/4 and 1/9 per chain.
Fencing upkeep — ,, 1/– and 2/6 per chain.

## SMALLHOLDINGS

There were now 103 tenancies, and a sample of the census taken on 29th September is included here.

| NAME OF FARM | ORIGINAL LETTING | | | | | | PRESENT LETTING (1938) | | | | | |
| | AREA (ACRES) | NO. IN FAMILY | STOCK | | | | AREA | NO. IN FAMILY | STOCK | | | |
| | | | SHEEP | CATTLE | PIGS | HORSES | | | SHEEP | CATTLE | PIGS | HORSES |
|---|---|---|---|---|---|---|---|---|---|---|---|---|
| Llanerch Elsi | 161 | 4 | 160 | 16 | 1 | 1 | 127 | 2 | 96 | 4 | — | 1 |
| Mynydd Bychan | 248 | 4 | 200 | 20 | 1 | 1 | 57 | 5 | 50 | 7 | — | — |
| Rhiwgri | 74 | 2 | 70 | 4 | 1 | — | 70 | 1 | 64 | — | — | — |
| Maesnewyddion | 146 | 3 | 120 | 12 | 1 | 2 | 98 | 3 | 90 | 1 | — | — |
| Cae'n y Coed | 32 | 3 | 40 | 6 | — | — | 32 | 5 | — | — | — | — |
| Craig Forys | 105 | 4 | 80 | 10 | 1 | — | 24 | 5 | 40 | 2 | — | — |
| Bryn Fawnog | 121 | 7 | 200 | — | — | — | 4 | 3 | — | — | — | — |
| Haffoty Pencraig | 90 | 6 | 100 | 4 | 1 | 1 | 82 | 2 | 60 | 7 | 1 | 1 |
| Fedw Deg | 228 | 2 | 245 | 15 | — | 1 | 32 | 3 | 50 | 4 | 1 | 1 |
| Penybryn | 386 | 3 | 250 | 25 | 2 | 2 | 141 | 5 | 120 | 15 | — | 1 |
| Tanaeldroch | 105 | 5 | 40 | 4 | 1 | 1 | 49 | 2 | 30 | 4 | 1 | 1 |

The majority of these farms and holdings are situated at fairly high elevations. The general decline in area is attributed to the gradual release of rough mountain grazing land to the Forestry Commission for afforestation; this was in accord with prescriptions outlined in the acquisition reports.

As the forest year drew to a close sinister events were shaping in Europe. It seemed as though the great May fire presaged impending clamour and chaos: the world appeared to be waiting, poised, alert and straining, aware of a murmuring menace that had risen to a roaring threat. And for the first time, when workmen's wives met in the streets the emphasis was not on 'Is George cutting coppice today?', but in solemn undertones: 'Did you hear the latest about this man Hitler, then?'.

The forest scene was dominated by the impending menace of war.

THREE HUNDRED AND EIGHTEEN ACRES WERE PLANTED IN 1939, the principal concentration being in High Parc, involving replanting of areas lost in the huge fire of the previous year. This planting was done between the former rows of piteously charred victims of the ravage, their skeletal lateral branches outflung in stark supplication over the stricken landscape, as though lamenting the blackened waste. A cold wind blew through the sombre aisles as the men replanted the area.

In the High Parc area there was a serious attack by *Strophosomus coryli*, a hazel weevil, on freshly planted spruce, and intensive trapping had to be resorted to throughout much of the summer before the infestation was arrested. As this weevil had never before been encountered in Gwydyr plantations, specimens were sent to an Oxford entomologist for identification and probable cause of presence. It was considered that by the destruction in the fire of all available food and breeding material (hazel, bilberry, etc.), *Strophosomus* had recourse to spruce as an alternative host. There has been no recorded evidence of a recurrence since this occasion.

War with Germany was declared, after a final ultimatum had been ignored, on Sunday, 3rd September, 1939.

GWYDYR FOREST'S SECOND DECADE ENDED IN 1940, the year of deliverance from Dunkirk, and in Sir Winston Churchill's own words, 'Britain's finest hour'.

It was a quiet, uneventful year in the forest. Two hundred and twenty-one acres were planted without mishap; the summer was a pleasant one and heavy bracken weeding was necessary. During the late summer period, the crisis succeeding Dunkirk and the evacuation to British shores of the bulk of our armies, involved the formation of Local Defence Volunteers (later, the Home Guard). Within a very few days of the initial call for volunteers many forestry men had joined. The function of this voluntary force was to organise defence of their particular area against saboteurs and parachutists, and in the event of invasion, to support army formations in tactical and strategical defence and counter-attack. Here, at Gwydyr, in this wild, wide, broken terrain, were men including gamekeepers, sheepfarmers, foresters and poachers, who knew every inch of the country, every forest aisle, and every cave and niche in the rocks. They would, if assailed, have given a good account of themselves. During the hours of daylight, forest staff engaged in operations on the uplands, were instructed to observe all aircraft movements, and to report anything suspicious.

## THE SECOND DECADE – CONCLUSIONS

Four thousand and seventy-seven acres had been planted, though some 240 acres of this total involved the replanting of areas lost through fire.

### CHOICE OF SPECIES

After 1937, European larch planting was discontinued. This was a logical decision considering all the unfavourable responses this species had exhibited over the years. Plainly it just did not contribute economically as a major forest species on the type of terrain existing at Gwydyr. Gorse competition had certainly impeded its early development and the exposure factor was also significant. Nonetheless, there were a few good areas, particularly in High Parc and parts of Cefn Manllwyd.

The restriction of Norway spruce to the better grass/bracken/ heather sites became standard after 1938; this reflected on the extensive use of this species in lieu of Sitka spruce and pines during the late-twenties and early-thirties, when both these species were often in such very short supply.

Lodgepole pine was being used much more on the rockier gorse/heather/*Molinia* knolls, and its response on the poorest plantable ground was better than other pines. The Silver firs in Miner's Bridge – planted in 1927 – were clearly successful and the prospect of utilising this species on similar sites was worth considering.

### FIRE

With the extension of the forest area the fire risk had increased enormously, though preventive and control measures had become more efficient. Patrolmen had developed a sense of real responsibility and urgency; local residents had become very co-operative in reporting smoke. The disastrous Parc fire of 1938 had its origin in a tramp's moment of thoughtlessness and the stifling of this conflagration exhausted every single helper. For the supervisory staff, the crop of fires in 1938 brought mental as well as physical weariness; the continual alerts, reconnoitring, actual fire-fighting directing, and the aftermath of reports and inquests was a strain on all. But the flood of voluntary help at these fires, from people outside the Forestry Commission, was at once heartening and comforting: it showed, at least, an increasing sense of responsibility. People just didn't flock around staring in aimless wonder and curiosity, but made a real contribution in the effort to get the fires under control.

Sheep trespass had been the subject of long standing contention.

Fencing, gates, hurdles, wall-stakes and barb wire, and high stone walls were all impediments to entry of sheep to planted areas. Yet they kept getting in; their wool would be found adhering to the top strand of barb on a $7\frac{1}{2}$-foot wall stake; they squeezed through a nine-inch gap between corner-posts and rock profiles; they bestrode narrow ledges on rock outcrops with the sure-footedness of mountain goats; and secured access to plantation areas by means not far short of gyration.

They developed into notorious jumpers. They were wild, wily and seemingly wise. It may seem erroneous to accord them the gift of wisdom, but somehow this seems more proper than ascribing it as a highly developed instinct.

To illustrate this. Just outside the Diosgydd nursery perimeter a gate was maintained across the public roadway. This was kept closed all the time workmen were engaged in the nursery, and any stray sheep observed by them were chased away. The sheep became wary; they kept a discreet distance and watched. They saw the men leaving work at the appointed time, observed them mounting their bicycles or walking off homewards down the mountain road; they saw the gate shut tight on its latch. Silence then, and the sheep would look at one another as though to confirm among themselves: 'Good, that's them out of the way. C'mon.' And, feet pattering, they would amble up to the gate and huddle there – perhaps three, or half a dozen, sometimes more. Huddle and wait patiently. And presently, up the road would come the visitors, perspiring and exclaiming in the late afternoon sunshine. They saw the sheep waiting outside the gate in a compact little group. As they came closer the sheep moved off a yard or so, bunched and unalarmed, watching them. 'They must be waiting to pass through the gate,' exclaim our visitors innocently, and delighted at the opportunity, open the gate and allow the sheep to precede them through. Within thirty seconds those sheep have leaped the fence and are in the nursery, and the head forester suspends his meal to go and hound them out, harbouring unkind thoughts towards irresponsible ramblers!

This didn't happen once or twice or a dozen times; it became a summertime ritual. Those sheep knew. When forestry employees were around they kept well away from the access point. But as soon as the men departed, the sheep gathered patiently and expectantly, knowing strangers would be along presently and the gate would be opened for them and all would be well. Instinct? Habit? Wisdom?

54

Prescience? Call it what you will, these sheep persisted in this practise for a very long time and over many seasons.

One particularly irksome ram, with a broken left horn, was cornered one day at Diosgydd nursery, when a lorry was loading plants for another forest fifteen miles away. The foreman, using desperate measures, told two men to tie the ram's legs together and place him securely in the lorry among the plants; the load was then covered with a tarpaulin. The driver was instructed to free the ram at a point just short of his destination, and outside the forest boundary. And with a sigh of relief, the foreman watched the lorry trundle off down the mountain road – conveying the ram to fresh pastures. The driver (it was later learnt) complied with his instructions, cutting the thongs and releasing the ram a mile short of the lorry's destination. The ram, puzzled and a little incommoded, ambled off across open ground, pausing now and then to sample the browse. Within six days he was back outside Diosgydd nursery gate, as large as life, awaiting the opportune moment to recontinue his depredations. Of such pertinacity are the Gwydyr sheep disposed!

A number of adjacent sheep owners were quite accomplished at assisting their sheep to gain entry into planted areas . . . and not always by deliberately leaving gates open or pushing down the odd length of stone wall. One was apprehended lifting a chunky young ram over a fenceline; surprised, nonplussed and thoroughly discomfited, his countenance took on a stricken appearance!

There were many access points for stray sheep outside Forestry Commission control. They could, and did, wander up through the main street in Betws-y-coed, and then take to one or another of the minor roads leading up through the plantations. Several local farmers did not appear at all concerned at numbers of their sheep wandering about through the planted areas; nor were they altogether co-operative in rounding them up! Only at lambing time was any urgency shown. It was not always easy to reconcile this outlook of theirs, for sheep, running free, were exposed to disease and injury on a scale far greater than they could experience within the confines of their home grazing grounds. Countless sheep were lost through getting caught up in dense bramble thickets and being unable to extricate themselves; others plunged into old, partially concealed mine-shafts or slipped over cliffs; untended lambs, born in the plantation depths, fell victims to foxes and birds of prey.

Forestry trappers saved scores of sheep from imminent death throughout plantation areas; they did a great deal to try and control this seemingly endless sheep trespass. But the vast areas

55

involved, and the complex nature of the terrain, made their duty both arduous and thankless.

## VERMIN

Rabbits were still the principal scourge to newly planted areas. They had been particularly troublesome on Diosgydd Uchaf, Tyddyn-du, Dol-Gochyn and Craig Forys. These locations were methodically ferreted after enclosure, but the odd rabbit seemingly always survived. The terrain was always in their favour, and 100% elimination whether by ferreting, shooting or snaring was well-nigh impossible.

Badgers did some damage to fences in the Lledr valley, Hafod-yr-ewen, and at Wyddfyd. Generally, however, the forester respected these animals, and the provision of a 'badger gate' at appropriate places on the 'walk' eliminated further trouble.

Hares were generally erratic in their incursions into young planted areas. They did sporadic damage to spruce and pine in the Glasgwm valley (P.36), and on Hafodgwenllian (P.34), during the February snowfall of 1937.

Generally though, considering the extent of the area of plantation encroaching into their upland habitat, damage was relatively low.

## LABOUR

Since the first decade this had very much improved. The advent of the second World War (1939) would doubtlessly mean a loss to the forest of the younger, able-bodied men. All the holdings were filled, though there was, after 1939, the possibility of a few tenants being transferred to holdings at other forests, at their own request.

## THINNINGS

Extraction of timber from many locations approaching the thinning stage was going to be difficult due to the steep slopes and the rock outcrop in most of the compartments. Horse extraction had been done in some areas already thinned. Careful study would be needed in siting economical extraction routes, and the possibility of utilising wire-ropes for extraction would require consideration.

## THE FOREST IMPACT

After 1937, Gwydyr had become a National Forest Park. Increasing numbers of visitors were arriving, both to motor or walk through the forest and to view the famed beauty spots adjacent to it. The war, however, with petrol rationing imminent, restricted the use of motor vehicles for pleasure.

Machno Vale and Pen-y-Bryn, Penmachno.

## Chapter 5

# THE THIRD DECADE: CONSOLIDATION

## 1941–1950

"... That I might drink and leave the world unseen
And with thee fade far away into the forest dim.
Fade far away, dissolve and quite forget
What thou amongst the leaves hast never known
The weariness, the fever and the fret,
Here, where men sit and hear each other groan."

Ode to a Nightingale, *John Keats*

War raged in Europe, Asia and Africa throughout the first half of the decade. Planting dropped from 210 acres in 1942 to only 11 acres in 1946 – the lowest ever recorded in the history of the forest. But timber production increased as the needs of war and the interests of

57

silvicultural practice yielded returns from expanding areas of thinnings. Extraction of timber and poles presented many problems at first. Early trials included 8-gauge galvanised wire ropeways, followed by steel cables and pulley blocks. Plantations were scoured during 1942–45 for special-sized poles to comply with service requirements, and for ladder-poles for the Fire Service, to replace thousands lost in the cities during air-raids. Specific industries sought special produce sizes, and the forest's contribution was significant and estimable. Although a reserved occupation, forestry nevertheless subscribed to conscription by releasing many of its younger able-bodied personnel for duties with the services. Gwydyr contributed over twenty to the cause and for the first time employed female labour to replace the loss in manpower. These women performed excellent service during the crisis.

Consolidation would seem to aptly describe this particular decade. The forest – established only after three years after one world war – now endured the second. It was welded, timber-production-wise in yielding up many of its fruits of those early years, and potential-wise in its rapid surge forward in expansion of plantations after 1946. It loomed defiant in its foothold stronghold. Home Guardsmen trained within its broad acres and maintained vigilance over valley and upland. Evacuated schoolboys from London performed valuable part-time work in its plantations. Recuperating soldiers, based on a locally requisitioned hotel, prospered in their recovery by walking along its footpaths. Gwydyr bestowed much to many in a time of great national stress.

And when the tide of war rolled away, spent and subdued, forest life resumed its normal routine, consolidating both its influence and its impacts.

There were many strange faces in the villages around the forest. Evacuated families from London, the Midlands and Lancashire took up residence in guest houses, etc., to escape the widespread bombing during 1941 and 1942. Dulwich Preparatory School took over the famous Royal Oak Hotel in Betws-y-Coed, and were soon in contact with local forest officials to enquire whether they could assist in any way as a contribution to the war effort. Parties of boys were engaged on two half-days a week to undertake brashing, or the low-pruning of conifer stands, and quickly became adept at this work. They were paid a small sum and got through a relatively large brashing programme from 1941 to 1943. In 1942 a small plot of Western hemlock was established beneath Japanese larch planted in 1921 behind Coedcynhelier, and the Dulwich boys planted this.

THE SEASON OF 1941 had a modest yet far-flung planting

programme – from Crafnant in the north, Bryn Engan in the west, and Penmachno in the south. Operations commenced in the Capel Curig area – the Bryn Engan acquisition contained a very useful cover of oak over a large part of the lower slopes, and this was of high amenity attractiveness since it flanks the Holyhead road, A.5. The oak was of good form and density considering the terrain, and formed a pleasant visual feature; the 1941 programme however did not involve this but the land immediately opposite the Llynau Mymbyr (Mymbyr Lakes). This was a former sheep 'mountain' and the bulk of the ground preparation comprised the cutting of dense blackthorn clumps and the removal of the poorest form of oak and birch scrub, retaining only those trees of good form. Extensive draining was necessary.

At Hafod Dwryd (Penmachno) ploughing was introduced for the first time in Gwydyr Forest. Although reasonably successful, the broken nature of the uplands and the absence of a long economical run made it questionable whether ploughing of such areas was really worth while. Tractors were far less developed than they are today and had none of the adaptations for traction on plateau and bog sites. Still, it was a start, and however modest the success, much experience was gained in terms of economy and adaptability.

In the Soflen Woods there was much selective clearing of scrub, undergrowth and coppice to be undertaken; there was no question of cutting away all the good cover. The intention was to plant Douglas fir and Western hemlock through hazel underwood, merely achieving sufficient direct overhead clearance for the trees to develop. Later, a gradual thinning out of the overwood would proceed. Establishment was very successful indeed. On the more open sites Japanese larch and Norway spruce were used.

Lord Robinson, Chairman of the Forestry Commission, visited the forest in 1941, concentrating his interests on the subject of underplanting Japanese larch areas. He advised that three plots should be treated in this fashion:

(a) The Japanese larch thinned normally.
(b) The plot area fenced.
(c) All undergrowth cleared.
(d) Underplanting with Western hemlock at five feet spacing.

As a consequence it was decided to establish these plots at Coedcynhelier, Maesnewyddion and Pen-y-parc, and in 1942 all three plots were duly treated as prescribed. It became apparent however, in 1945, that the Western hemlock would require more than an ordinary thinning of the larch canopy if they were to develop satisfactorily. In one of the plots – Maesnewyddion – a much heavier thinning of the larch was undertaken in 1946, and the remaining were similarly treated in 1947. Response since has been excellent.

In Diosgydd plantation, established in 1921, the Douglas fir and European larch were ready for thinning. Extraction of the poles was the principal problem as the nature of the rocky terrain and size of produce made economical horse extraction problematical. After much trial and tribulation a wire-rope system was introduced, using 8-gauge galvanised fence wire, and an extraction run of 300 yards was achieved. This was a giant stride forward though there were still snags to iron out – wire tension factors, balancing the load correctly, securing the produce, etc. Gradually a new approach led to increased improvement and efficiency with the use of steel cables and pulleys. Output soared and extraction costs fell, and enthusiastic forest staff began looking at further sites to apply their pulley and steel cable system . . . pioneer experiments of this nature will always bring moments of triumph and delight.

THE YEAR 1942 brought a reduced planting accomplishment (210 acres) and also the forest's first experience of bombs. In the early hours of a May morning a 'stick' of five bombs descended on the Glyn area, between Ty'n Llwyn holding and Bodgynydd lake. Very little damage to trees was experienced and none to property, and no resultant fire was started. No one seemed to know quite why these bombs should have fallen where they did – we certainly had no national treasures or secret weapons secured away in this fastness – but the concensus of opinion at the time was either (a) indifferent navigation, (b) the crew were deceived by the glittering moonlight reflected on the lake's surface and considered it a worthwhile target. If so the crew must have numbered several indifferent members, for the bomb-aimer was as wayward as his navigator and the stick fell a long way off the presupposed target. No British planes were in pursuit at the time. Late in June two bombs fell on Hadfodlas quarry – here again a somewhat capricious achievement, but fortunate in that no loss of life or property was involved.

One large fire outbreak was experienced during this year; 108 acres were lost, some over ground involved in the Parc fire of 1938.

THE PERIOD 1943–46 continued the restraint in extensive plantings. This was fully justified in the light of other commitments. Selected poles, pitwood and special timber produce size-ranges occupied much of the men's time.

*Plate 15.* A striking view of the Llugwy Gorge close to the Swallow Falls, looking south from Craig-yr-Hafod on the North bank.

*Plate 16.* Llyn-y-Parc.

*Plate 17.* Lledr Valley, looking west towards Moel Siabod.

Of the planting achieved over this 4-year period the following figures illustrate the decline in acreage:

1943   75 acres.   Ty Nant (Gwibernant) and Hafod Dwryd (Penmachno).

1944   34 acres   Crafnant and Cwm Dreiniog.

1945   25 acres.   Crafnant and Alltwen mountain (part replanting after the 1942 fire).

1946   11 acres.   Nant and Alltwen mountain.

On Crafnant the planting range was being extended well above the heights reached in the original establishment year (1937). It was a difficult site – on broken hill slopes with terraces, rock outcrops and boggy depressions. A lot of draining and turfing was required. On Alltwen, reafforestation of part of the area lost in the 1942 fire was begun, whilst at Cwm Dreiniog planting pushed out towards the vicinity of Elsi lake.

The total staff employed in the forest in late 1944 numbered 93 males and 10 females. All the holdings were in occupation; many older employees had now been in the forest for twenty years or more and a few of their sons were entering the service.

When war ceased in 1945 a gradual transformation commenced – the emphasis was now shifting to thinning and timber production. More and more plantations were coming into the first thinning stage; similarly older sites were now available for second and subsequent thinnings. Horse and tractor extraction routes were being planned. There were whisperings of the introduction of a forest road system. The advantages were all too obvious, both for extraction and fire protection, but much of the terrain was of an extremely difficult nature and would entail considerable blasting.

IN 1947 the planting programme soared to 328 acres. This was the year of a really severe winter, followed by an exceptionally prolonged, dry summer. As a consequence of this marked seasonal contrast, two operations – planting and weeding – were protracted into early May and early October respectively. Fire risk throughout the season was acute, there were many alarms along the notorious Lledr valley railway stretch and three potentially serious outbreaks were averted by prompt and disciplined action.

Despite an acute shortage of planting stock during 1948, the acreage completed rose to 427 acres. The smallholding of Garth Eryr was planted up, and a part of Cae Huddygl. The former holding had become vacant after a tenure of 27 years and much of the land available was rough mountain grazing on the fringe of Elsi Lake plateau. The small island feature in Sarnau Lake was planted up with Scots and Lodgepole pines and Sitka spruce, and would in future contribute considerable scenic merit to an otherwise bleak prospect.

After a long association, reaching back to the forest's inception in 1921, Diosgydd nursery was closed down. Over 15 million seedlings and transplants had been raised and despatched from this nursery over its twenty-seven years' life. Thus, a significant link with the past was severed and a colourful chapter closed – for the nursery had sentimental attachment to many who had been associated with it down the years. Many distinguished visitors had trod its paths and surveyed the stock in the lines. Many an animated scene had been witnessed as lorries queued for loading, and men scurried back and forth with barrowloads of plants. Many thousands of holiday-makers had admired the neat rows of plants and commented on their display. But the trend was to utilise larger nurseries, where mechanisation could flourish and access would be easier. Further-more the soil in Diosgydd was becoming impoverished. So the long race was run. Out in the plantations however – on heatherclad plateau and steep sided valley – the babes from the nursery were growing in stature, a positive and triumphant tribute to the nursery's past.

A Forester Training School was established on the premises of the former Ministry of Labour training camp at Glyn. A section of the forest was set aside as a 'school beat' and was administered as a separate management unit.

THE YEAR 1949 saw a decline in the total planted area to 322 acres. Plantations were extended at Bryn Engan, Ty'n y Cwm and Cwm Celyn. On deep peat in the Bwlch (Dolwyddelan) the area was ploughed, and planted with 46,000 two-year old well-rooted Sitka spruce seedlings. Growth started well, but during June drought the 'cheesy' peat furrow slices cracked open and plant roots were exposed, resulting in moderate losses. On a ploughed heather site on the same area, Scots pine was used with Sitka spruce in a single row mixture and established well. Frustration with the plough was experienced on locations where the rock level lay only a few inches beneath the heather or where rock outcrops occurred. These impeded long economic runs and caused much re-alignment of plough furrows.

In June of this year the Society of Irish Foresters paid a visit to the forest. An extract from the Irish press coverage of this tour is an enlightening commentary:

'The Irish Society of Foresters' visit to North Wales was tremen-dous value ... North Wales is an ill-favoured territory. The

Where the Llugwy joins the Conway, looking towards Capel Garmon from Betws-y-Coed.

Forestry Commission had courage; the vast rough country with the great elevations and complex geology, the poor soils and the high rainfall is now furnished with coniferous forests. The forest follows the natural features of the rugged countryside and makes the unsightly, poor places seem rich and beautiful. Betws-y-Coed unsightly? Yes, remove the trees and leave the harsh outline and what have you? An unprofitable wilderness – no nation is so rich that it can afford such scenery in these times of world scarcity . . . if it were not for the afforestation Betws-y-Coed would be as bleak and neglected as Maam Cross, back in Ireland.'

'We liked the moorland best. Our men spread out, examined the characteristic flora and heeled up the underlying earth. There were great debates on whether we had, or had not, land as poor as this at home. For the ordinary man not directly concerned with making forestry land out of wastes it was sufficient to pass from the healthy stands of spruce and pine to the open, unplanted, areas with the cover of cotton grass and deer-grass. Truly the newly introduced conifers are a boon to these islands. We can have timber now where once nothing profitable would grow!'

THE THIRD DECADE CLOSED with a surging impetus in acreage planted. Six hundred and fifty-five acres were completed in 1950, including large areas at Bwlch-y-Maen, where on ploughed heather ground Scots pine was used with Sitka spruce in row mixture, Hendre Buarthau and Ty'n-y-Cwm.

One interesting feature should be emphasised at this stage – the emergence of the second generation of forest workers. These were the sons and relations of many of the original tenants. They had grown up on the smallholdings and farms within the forests. They had become inured to the forest scene, walking through plantations on their way to school. Smallholders are a tight-knit, constrained community, and the youths were acutely influenced by their fathers. Many left school in their mid-teens when the prospect of employment in the forest was assured. They replaced fathers and uncles who had achieved, or were fast approaching, retirement age. Thus a forest continuity was effected, nearly thirty years after the forest's establishment. It held significance in that a tradition was being instigated, a subtle awakening to the impact of the forest environment.


THE THIRD DECADE – CONCLUSIONS

Two thousand, three hundred and fifty-three acres were planted, a worthy achievement considering half the period involved the nation in war.

## THINNING

Third thinnings of Douglas fir on Diosgydd and Norway spruce and Douglas fir in Maesnewyddion had been completed. A heavier-than-normal intervention had to be undertaken in these plantations in the quest for suitable and adequate quantities of timber of special war requirements. Wire ropeways had contributed considerably to economical extraction, particularly on steep boulder-strewn slopes; their success at Gwydyr prompted their introduction on other forests in North Wales. However, it was evident that other means of hauling out timber would have to be evolved as annual thinning areas rose, and volumes increased. Many inhospitable sites on the plateau land were entering thinning stages – and these involved carefully selected produce extraction routes, with as regular a gradient as possible.

## BRASHING

Large areas had been brashed, that is, low-pruned, reducing the fire risk on certain particularly dangerous sites. Except for misshapen and really dominated trees a full brashing was undertaken. Inspection tracks for the forest staff probed into many remote areas – on the really steep and difficult slopes these proved highly advantageous.

## PLANTING AND PLANT SUPPLIES

Planting totals were the lowest for the three decades. The intervention of war, however, influenced this, as did shortages of suitable young trees. Replanting of those areas of High Parc lost in the great 1938 fire was completed in 1941.

## CLEANING THE YOUNG PLANTATIONS

This was still the principal maintenance operation. Though little of it was necessary to accomplish a thorough programme of cleaning in the Carreg Gwalch and Craig Glan Conway plantations, among fifteen-year old conifers, during 1941 and 1942 – birch being the principal weed tree.

## VISUAL AMENITY

It was becoming increasingly clear that in the Lledr and Llugwy valleys – areas of high aesthetic appeal – the retention of intermittent oak scrub, the establishment of broadleaved belts, and the careful blending of species was of special significance in the visual scene. There was an absence, in effect, of any artificially-created forest effect, so well did the plantations blend in with their rugged backcloths. Locally, the residents had come to accept the forest presence and there were few dissonant voices raised in criticism. On the upper forest levels, too, plantations had developed sufficiently to enhance the moorland views. Gwydyr had shed much of its growing pains in terms of adverse public comment.

Near Trefriw, Conway Valley.

## Chapter 6

# THE FOURTH DECADE: MECHANISATION

1951-1960

"There is a pleasure in the pathless woods
. . . I love not men the less, but nature more,
From these our interviews. . . ."

*Byron*

AT GWYDYR, IN 1951, heavy plant machinery moved in to
commence the forest road programme. Ploughing of the upland
areas became common practice wherever possible – the age of the
machine emerged, and violated the one-time sanctity of the forest
fastnesses.

Many of the upland forest holdings became vacant with the exodus of the older-established tenants to council houses in the surrounding hamlets, and the difficulty in replacing them. Some smallholdings were resumed for planting; others were to be let as summer cottages.

In many ways the pattern of the smallholding communities was altering. Close-knit for thirty-odd years; fully occupied during the build-up of the forest; now a gradual decline became apparent. Houses and outbuildings stood deserted and lonely; no voices broke the sullen silence brooding over the empty pastures and the patch-work of grey stone walls.

A phase of the forest scene was being immersed into history – only the ghosts of old-time tenants haunted the forlorn habitations:

> "All within is dark as night
> In the window is no light
> And no murmur at the door
> So frequent on its hinge before."

> —The deserted house— *Tennyson*.

IN THE YEAR 1951 627 acres of new planting were completed over widespread areas – Bryn Engan, Upper Hafodgwenllian, Bwlch, Pen-y-Benar, Cwm Penmachno and Gelli in the Crafnant valley. On the last-named site an overwood of mixed hardwoods was retained for shelter and scenic effect and such trees as Red cedar, Douglas fir and Red oak were introduced beneath its cover. Planting conditions were good and resulted in high survival. 92·48 inches of rainfall was recorded for the twelve months, at Capel Curig – August (10·8″) and September (10·71″) were particularly wet.

Planning staff undertook intensive road surveys and a road gang was formed. A loop road was begun on the Glyn, after the fire of 12th May. Bulldozers appeared on the plateau lands for the first time and the plantations echoed to the cannonades of blasting through rock. Ribbons of road-cut extended slowly through the Parc Lake region, across sites once ravished by the 1938 fire. This was the birth of a new forest activity, the workings of an ancillary organisation, the onset of mechanisation . . . a prelude to a large future expansion of essential forest arteries which would reach to the remotest plantations.

Rabbits persisted and 531 were destroyed during the year. Many were found higher up on the moorland areas than a decade ago – indicative, perhaps, of favourable fresh sites where the younger plantations had not yet formed complete canopy, as was now the position on most of the lower valley slopes and the fringes of the upland areas. The Diosgydd-Alltwen-Penrallt triangle was still heavily infested, despite concentrated trapping.

An indication of the extent of new works programmes for the year can be ascertained from the following figures: 11,836 chains of new drains, 758 chains of new fencing. Much of this was on Pen-y-Bennar and Tan-y-Clogwyn. Five hundred and eighty-seven acres were thinned, yielding a total volume of 148,000 cubic feet, or a return of some 250 cubic feet per acre.

THE YEAR 1952 continued the large expansion of new plantations – 589 acres were planted. This programme was concentrated into three areas: Cwm Penmachno, Bwlch (near Dolwyddelan) and the Tan-yr-Eglwys – Cefn Manllwyd area of Nant mountain. The latter terrain comprised really difficult afforestation sites, involving much heather/*Myrica*/*Molinia* ground. Fortunately a fair measure of ploughing could be accomplished, leaving only the rock outcrops and thin-soiled zones for pre-planting operations by hand. Completion of planting here linked up with much older plantations to the south, south-west and east.

More bulldozers and road equipment were moved into the forest. Due to rock outcrops, much drilling and explosive work was necessary. Road construction in this terrain was to be a formidable undertaking, as a gradient not steeper than 1 in 10 was imperative.

On the timber production side the average volume per acre cut increased to 370 cubic feet, an increase of some 120 cubic feet per acre on 1951 figures. A total of 554 acres were thinned, realising an output of 205,070 cubic feet.

IN CORONATION YEAR, 1953, a total of 655 acres was planted in the forest – the principal concentration being on Carn-y-Parc and Bennar mountain (Penmachno), and at Ty'n-y-Berth in the Lledr Valley. Here, high amenity considerations had to be resolved and careful plantation lay-out observed. Species chosen included Red oak and beech. At Penmachno 140 acres were ploughed successfully. The burnt Glyn was replanted and $1\frac{1}{2}$ ounces of ground mineral phosphate applied to every tree there, and at Bennar, on the very poorest sites.

It was a year of whimsical and capricious weather contrasts. Mid-December had two days of severe gales whereby small pockets of windblow occurred in Maesnewyddion (Sitka spruce and Douglas fir planted in 1922) and Diosgydd (Douglas fir planted in 1922). Nowhere was damage extensive, being confined mainly to trees on rock ledges or on heavy clay soils in depressions, where soil aeration and drainage was poor. But it presaged likely future inroads into such woods. It highlighted and emphasised the impact of these channelled valley winds and their action on sixty-foot-plus conifers established on terraces and ledges with such thin soil cover and inadequate root anchorage.

Between the following 31st January and the 3rd February, further gales of severe force struck the forest and more individual and small groups of trees were blown in the same areas, and also on the Glyn (Norway spruce, planted 1930), Hafodgwenllian (Norway spruce, planted 1933), and Coed-y-Wern (Douglas fir, planted 1930).

No rain fell between 25th February and 25th March – the longest dry spell for seventeen years. Adjoining farmers took this opportunity to burn off heather and gorse on the moorlands, and there occurred a prolonged fire-danger period. April came in cold and remained so for about three weeks; the Douglas fir on Ty'n-y-Berth became badly browned and there were nearly 70% casualties.

Comparative rainfall figures for the year show the wide differences usual for Gwydyr's varied terrain.

| | | |
|---|---|---|
| Measured at Llanrwst | | 48 inches |
| ,, at Beddgelert | | 94 inches |
| ,, on Snowdon (summit) | | 200 inches |
| ,, Blaenau Ffestiniog | | 104 inches |
| ,, Colwyn Bay | | 29 inches. |

Road-making was concentrated on High Parc and a beginning was made on the access bridge at Bryn Engan.

A total of 97,950 cubic feet of timber was cut as thinnings.

THE YEAR 1954 was characterised by a very wet, dismal summer, and a consequent less-than-average fire-danger season. From June to September there was an average of 24 wet days per month. During February, 14 successive frosty nights occurred – 28 degrees of frost were recorded, and ink froze solid in the inkwells in the forest office.

Planting totalled 481 acres and included extending the plantations on Bryn Engan and the replanting of the area west of Parc lake, burnt in the fire of 1942. Lawson cypress was introduced on some of the heather sites here; it was planted in mixture with Scots pine in April, when soil and weather conditions were very dry, and this resulted in a high mortality rate.

By the end of the forest year 5½ miles of road had been completed. Much use was being made of drilling and explosives in these rocky, upland areas, but progress was steady despite poor weather conditions. Two thousand, five hundred and forty-six chains of drains were completed and the thinning total of 477 acres realised 116,101 cubic feet of timber.

On the areas at Gwibernant and Tan-yr-Allt, planted in 1940 and 1943, much cleaning of overhanging hardwood was accomplished. This had to be treated with detailed attention as there were visual amenity considerations to accept.

There was a gradual departure of the older-established forest tenants from the upland farm holdings to council houses in villages nearby. These scattered holdings had been of considerable significance during the formative years of the forest, particularly with regard to the multiple land-use aspect and the deployment of labour. The plateau lands and the upper fringes of the valley slopes had contained a fairly high population in these holdings – the average figure throughout the late twenty's and thirties being about five per house – and many children had attended the isolated school at Nant Bwlch-y-Haiarn. But now the emphasis shifted; deserted holding land was taken up for planting; families broke away from the traditional homesteads and moved down into the valleys; attendance at the Nant school slumped, and the role of the forest smallholder and farm holdings no longer subscribed such an impact to the forest scene. Perhaps this was an inevitable step, but the forest lost something in the process.

For the first time within the forest, decimation of the rabbit population through myxomatosis was observed in outlying blocks in the lower Conway valley.

THE 1955 planting programme involved relatively small, scattered areas stretching from Glyn Parc (near Ro Wen) to Mur Coch, in Dolwyddelan. Two hundred and ninety-five acres were planted, of which 39 were of broadleaved species.

More than 40 inches of rain fell between October and December and this period was characterised by devastating gales. A total of 84·33″ was recorded for the year at the Gwydyr Forester Training School; a depressingly long wet summer was broken only by a fine spell in late July and into the third week of August.

Despite the fact that in one day ten lineside fires were fought in the Lledr valley, fire danger throughout the year was below average. A total of 2,843 chains of new draining was achieved, and 1,564 chains of fire-lines ploughed and hand cut.

Myxomatosis proved to be almost 100% effective throughout much of the forest and the use of 'surface-burrows' by rabbits was observed for the first time. Up to the end of the year, however, the disease had not spread to the upper 'ffridd' lands or the fringes of the moors.

A total of 436 acres of plantation were thinned yielding 144,103 cubic feet of timber or about 330 cubic feet per acre.

IN 1956, for the first time, the ratio of broadleaved planting to conifer rose to one-fifth, out of a total of 378 acres planted. The reason for this relatively high hardwood planting lay in the acquisition of small, detached blocks in the Conway and Crafnant valleys, with consequent better soils and an emphasis on retaining as much of the hardwood character of the area as was reconcilable with economic land use. Amenity played a large part in choice of species in Carreg Oleu, at Dolgarrog, Coed Tan Dderwen, Gelli, Coed Cae Huddygl and on the lower reaches of Mynydd Deulyn. Much beech was used – either pure or in mixture with Grand fir and Western hemlock – and *Nothofagus*, Red oak and poplars were introduced. On many sites the overwood was retained and much use made of the shade and partial shade-bearing qualities of species such as hemlock, Grand fir, Douglas fir and Lawson cypress.

It was the first year wherein the bulk of a planting programme was concentrated on small, detached derelict woodlands, in locations away from plateau or steep hillside sites.

From March onwards diesel locomotives were introduced on the Llandudno Junction–Blaenau Ffestiniog railway, thus almost eliminating the fire danger in the Lledr valley region, which had been a source of embarrassment and apprehension for overy thirty years. Financially it meant a saving in patrolling and in the preparation of screefed firelines. The local stationmaster maintained close liaison with the forest staff, who were informed immediately in the event of any steam train substitution becoming necessary at short notice.

Weather-wise, the year provided extreme contrasts. A prolonged spring drought ended with a severe frost on May 19th, with much damage to Japanese larch and Lawson cypress. A very wet late summer and autumn seriously hampered timber extraction and road operations.

It was a beech mast year – and a good one – and particularly heavy coning of the spruces, Douglas fir, Noble fir, Lawson cypress and Red cedar.

Nine smallholdings were abandoned, continuing the pattern set two years before. On the land acquisition side only small, scattered blocks – mainly derelict woodlands – were coming to hand.

IN 1957 only 99 acres of new ground was afforested, but 44 acres of underplanting of indifferent European larch were completed. Much of this was on the Diosgydd bank (planted in 1921), where the larch was heavily thinned and enriched with Western hemlock, beech, *Cryptomeria japonica* and Noble fir. The larch here had been slow to achieve reasonable growth, and though many showed poor form and indications of canker, the seventy or so trees retained on each acre were of tolerably good shape and could reasonably be expected to respond to fresh conditions. At Pentre-du and in the Lledr valley similar European larch areas were treated in the same way.

There was a severe spring drought this year, and newly planted Japanese larch unfortunately flushed early and fell victim to this long dry interlude. July and August were characterised by a more than average number of thunderstorms with torrential rain. The weather broke completely – one could hardly call it a summer at all. Horace Walpole was near the truth when he wrote that 'the way to ensure summer in our country is to have it framed and glazed in a comfortable room'.

A thinning programme of 639 acres was completed, with a yield of 240,194 cubic feet.

For the first time polythene bags were used for holding trees prior to planting in order to conserve moisture and lessen planting losses.

A plague of voles and mice was evident during late spring and early summer, and beech boles up to $1\frac{1}{2}''$ diameter were eaten through in Bryn Engan, Canol-yr-Allt, Dolgarrog and the Pandy Mills plantations. There appeared to be an increase in rabbit and hare population, and the initial impact of myxomatosis would seem to be on the wane. Isolated populations of rabbits on the 'ffridd' lands had escaped all contact with the infection and its horrid symptoms.

Four well-known holdings were vacated this year – Pen y Parc, Bryn Fawnog, Llidiart y Gwynt and Talaergerwyn. At one time or another all had accommodated 'characters' well known in the forest – tenants who through their respective characteristics had acquired repute – humorous, quixotic, stoical, loquacious. Two of these smallholdings had been occupied by men who had long experience of local lead mining, and some of their anecdotes would have chilled the hearts of even the most hardened Klondike campaigner.

On 4th September 1957, a tree planting ceremony to commemorate the planting by the Forestry Commission of the first 100,000 acres in North Wales, was held within the beautiful, cathedral-like setting of Artist's Wood. A commemorative stone was unveiled by the Rt. Hon. Henry Brook, M.P., Minister of Housing and Local Government and Minister for Welsh Affairs. Trees were planted to commemorate this achievement by the Minister, by Conservancy staff long associated with Gwydyr, and by a long-serving workman representing the forest staff. It was a significant and moving tribute to the Commission's achievements.

DURING 1958, 242 acres were planted. Once more the bulk of planting embraced detached blocks along the Conway Valley – Coed y Garth, Goed Fron Acre and Cefn Coch. In the Llugwy valley amenity considerations were taken into account when trees were chosen. A classic example of this can be observed in Coed Cae Huddygl today. Part of this wood had been treated and planted in 1956 and the remainder in 1957. It comprised a broadleaved mixture of inferior quality, uneconomic oak, birch, ash and sycamore, on a southerly aspect sloping down to the river Llugwy and the Swallow Falls and almost flanking the main Holyhead road, A.5. From the visual amenity aspect it was essential to preserve the hardwood character of the area and yet make economic use of the site by introducing conifers. The hardwoods were judiciously thinned out and groups of beech, *Nothofagus*, Douglas fir, Western hemlock and Grand fir introduced beneath the canopy; later, a gradual removal of some of the deciduous species would be necessary and the wood would assume a pleasing mixed pattern.

By the end of the year the total forest road length stood at 51 miles – the Glyn, High Parc, Maesnewyddion and Penrallt areas being reasonably well served. Six hundred and ninety-one acres were thinned, yielding 247,308 cubic feet, or about 358 cubic feet of timber per acre. Treatment of unproductive and low productive European larch areas continued with selective felling of 59 acres on Ffrith-Sian (planted in 1927) and subsequent enrichment with Douglas fir, Western hemlock and Red cedar. It was a good seed year. Thirty-one-year old Western hemlock, in Miner's Bridge, were laden, and sycamore and ash seed was plentiful. Vole damage was extensive once again, with beech, Lawson cypress and Red cedar the principal victims; much beating-up had to be resorted to.

Two workmen retired with a combined total of 68 years' service – both having begun at Gwydyr in 1924. They planted their contribution in the Artist's Wood commemoration plot. One had performed service as a trapper for the full 34 years and had rarely missed a day through indisposition, the other was one of the most versatile employees ever to have served here. Their contribution to the forests' development had been able, loyal and positive.

Reports tended to confirm that the badger population within the forest was on the increase. On part of the replanted Alltwen mountain – planted 1954 – barking on the stems of Sitka spruce was noticed. This was occurring about $2\frac{1}{2}$ feet above the ground and for many weeks puzzled observers who could not readily identify the cause of the damage, as fresh trees were being barked weekly. After incessant search and observation, the damage ceased when an eccentric ram with ingrowing horns was ejected from the plantation by one of the trappers.

DURING 1965 the two principal planting areas were at Gallt-y-Rhyg, where 115 acres were re-afforested, and in the Cyffty Mountain-Bryn Fawnog area on the plateau west of Llanrwst. Other small areas embraced a portion of Hafodgwenllian, and the planting of Coed Maenan, near Maenan Abbey, an area of high amenity significance. In all 270 acres were planted up.

It was an exceptionally dry, warm summer, causing much 'browning off' of some species. Fire protection was consequently very costly, with patrols duplicated at weekends along the more frequently-visited plantations; there were several urgent firecalls and alarms but no serious outbreaks.

A grey squirrel was observed within the forest perimeter for the first time, being located on the eastern (Denbighshire) side of the river Conway. A decrease in foxes was reported, though the rabbit population was increasing everywhere.

THE LAST YEAR OF THIS FOURTH DECADE, 1960, saw a marked decrease in planting. One hundred and six acres were planted, of which 64 acres involved re-afforestation, using 30% of hardwoods. This comparatively high proportion of broadleaved species was due to the acquisition of land near Llandudno Junction (Marl Hall) and at Coed Bryn-Garth, at Mochdre, on areas of limestone. On these sites much beech and Red oak was used; it was the first time in the forest's history for trees to be established on a dominating limestone soil, and completed the remarkably wide variation of soil types found within the forest.

January was very wet; 21 inches of rain fell on high ground during the month, and this cold, damp period persisted through February and into early March, delaying planting operations. During October snow appeared on the Snowdonian mountains and reached down to the upper forest levels; the rest of the autumn was wet and extremely windy. Lightning started a fire on the Crafnant area on Whit Sunday, but this was quickly suppressed; fire risk was generally low throughout the danger season. Arrangements were made with the local Fire Services to give a distinctive fire-call to distinguish forest fires from other fire sources; this would save many needless investigation journeys by forest staff.

Initial and second high thinnings of Norway and Sitka spruce showed that a profitable return could be achieved from early thinnings for pulpwood material.

It was disquietening to report an increase in sheep and rabbit damage during the year. Emphasis was stressed on renewing hill mountain boundaries over a cycle of years; this would involve a great deal of work and could only be accomplished gradually.

The forest road system was increasingly opening up plantations and the public were taking advantage of this. Many private vehicles were frequenting certain roads and there was need for firm, but tactful, restraint whenever they were encountered. Manifestly this was going to develop into an increasing problem over the years ahead.

## THE FOURTH DECADE – CONCLUSIONS

Three thousand, seven hundred and forty-two acres were established within the decade. This, however, includes the underplanting of certain heavily-thinned European larch woods. A higher percentage of broadleaved species – primarily beech, oak and Red oak – were utilised throughout the decade compared with previous years, due to higher site fertility on newly acquired areas and visual amenity grounds.

### ROADS

Road construction became a main feature in the decade's activities. Many established timber-producing areas had been reached and access to remote locations, in the event of fire outbreak, had been made easier.

### TIMBER PRODUCTION

Whole blocks of forest were now in the harvesting stage. Yield per acre overall was fairly consistent; on the plateau lands however, increment had been low, particularly on north and west aspects with moderate to severe exposure. Fortunately windblow had not been significant.

### FIRE

Other than the Glyn fire in May 1951, there had been no severe outbreaks. Fire danger was now diminishing in the valley areas of the Llugwy, Lledr and Machno, and was concentrated on the plateau locations where there was still much inflammable vegetation, both within the plantations and on adjacent, unplanted open stretches of moor and rough grazing ground. Communications were

*Plate 18.* Broad sweep of Conway Vale, viewed from hilltop south of Betws-y-Coed.

*Plate 19.* Small farms and young plantations on hills north-west of Betws-y-Coed.

*Plate 20.* Swallow Falls framed in oakwoods below Holyhead road. Unusual view from summit of Craig-yr-Hafod or Summer House Crag.

*Plate 21*. Snowdon viewed from Llynau Mymbyr, Capel Curig.

*Plate 22*. Llyn Bodgynydd.

*Plate 23.* Panorama: From Ty'n Llwyn picnic site on by-road linking Ugly House
with Llanrwst. Hill farms, Llugwy Gorge and far moorlands of Mynydd Hiraethog,
or Mountains of Memories, away in Denbighshire.

now more advanced than during any previous period in the forest's history and one could anticipate increased efficiency in the years ahead.

## PLOUGHING, PLANTING AND PLANT SUPPLY

All but rocky areas and the worst boggy zones at the higher forest levels, were now being ploughed which gave rise to quicker, more uniform establishment. It also reduced weeding costs and lowered the need to replace losses. Nevertheless all the acquired derelict woodlands and many upland ridge locations had to be hand-prepared. The plant requirements position had eased considerably and in only one or two seasons did a shortage of Sitka spruce and Lodgepole pine occur. Beech and Red oak were in good supply for amenity planting.

## PLANTATION MAINTENANCE

Coppice cleaning and the upkeep of drains continued to absorb much time and money. Now that many of the older plantations on the difficult plateau land were well established, it was imperative to concentrate on maintaining a free flow of water through the drainage systems to reduce the potential risk from windthrow.

## THE FOREST AND THE PUBLIC

Visitors were on the increase, and the encroaching tide of humanity on holiday sought ingress to plantations everywhere. Throughout woodlands bisected by minor council roads, the density of traffic increased at weekends and peak holiday periods. This impact, and its consequences, was an inevitable factor in the development of the forest. One could hardly foresee the full effects of this invasion; certainly there was no staying the public from participating in the popularity and appeal of Gwydyr's scenic merits.

F*

Snowdon from Capel Curig.

## Chapter 7

# THE FIFTH DECADE: ENDOWMENT

## 1961–1970

"One impulse from a vernal wood
May teach you more of man,
Of moral evil and of good
Than all the sages can."

*William Wordsworth.*

A fulfilment had been achieved by the end of this decade. The forest was yielding its valuable harvest; an abundant road system united its far-flung plantations; a vast influx of public had come to appreciate its wild, wide sweep of colour and beauty; the value of its amenities and recreational facilities became patently manifest.

Like a vast canvas, Gwydyr's plantations clothed the valley slopes, the crags and the broken moorlands. To a young generation, making their first contact with its broad sweep, the forest is a heritage. They came in awe and wonder and anticipation, exclaiming at its visual attraction, marvelling at its wide range of trees. The products of the forest evoked their interest; inquisitive minds probed and questioned. They came in rain and wind and sunshine – and not a few, in snowy squalls – and were rewarded. An older generation find comfort and tranquillity, and a deep sense of reverence. This, then is a measure of the Forestry Commission's achievements. Public acknowledgment and appraisement of nearly fifty years of endeavour may not be financially rewarding, or influential policy wise, but it is a sum of human emotion, which, more and more, will seek the forest's impact and be rewarded by its intimacy.

THE 1961 planting programme was scattered over smallish areas, involving derelict woodland sites and open moorland locations. One hundred and eighty-nine acres were completed including the re-planting of 69 acres of felled or heavily thinned larch woods. The latter were situated on upland sites, poor in soil quality, and established during the period 1928–1932. Growth-rate had tended to diminish of latter years and it was considered uneconomical to retain larch as a crop on these more exposed areas. On sites where heavy thinning was involved, some forty stems were retained per acre and the crop enriched with Sitka spruce.

A timber harvesting team was started on one Gwydyr beat (Llanrwst) and careful output costings kept. The planting season was generally wet, and a severe widespread late spring frost occurred on 27th May.

At Penmachno both hares and rabbits increased, and myxomatosis was now only evident in parts of the forest.

THE YEAR 1962 emphasised the increasing public awareness of the forest. The Conservator stressed this in his annual report, concluding with this significant comment: 'There is unlimited scope, in the Snowdonia National Park in particular, for popularising the work of the Forestry Commission, but it is impossible to develop this rich vein without additional money and probably staff.'

It was a rich vein indeed, for though the public were visually very aware of the forest, they had yet to be piloted to the acceptance of a forest tradition. They were by no manner or means fully forest conscious in the broader sense. They were unacquainted with the management and methods of the Forestry Commission or the realisation that Gwydyr, and other forest parks, had developed into rich and vital heritages, containing a wealth of educational, recreational and aesthetic aspects.

Three hundred and twenty-eight acres were replanted during the year and 214 acres afforested; the former areas comprised felled or heavily thinned larch plantations on the poorer ground.

During the year the last of the local slate quarries – that at Cwm Penmachno – closed down, and there were many applicants for employment in the forest. This sociological aspect repeated the position which arose when Hafodlas quarry, near Betws-y-Coed, and Rhos quarry at Capel Curig, closed many years before, when numbers of employees were absorbed into forestry – the only alternative source of employment available to them in the district.

The first opening-up of a seed stand of Japanese larch – planted in 1929 – took place over one acre alongside the A.5. The red squirrel population remained constant; one grey squirrel was shot in an outlying plantation on the Denbighshire side of the Conway.

THE YEAR 1963 was dominated by the severity of the winter, when ten weeks of frost and biting east winds followed an early January snowfall. There were iceflows in the river Conway for the first time in living memory. The severe frost conditions caused prolonged damage to Douglas fir, where trees in the five to ten year category were killed outright. Gorse, too, succumbed on every aspect, and added to the fire risk during late Spring.

Two hundred and twenty-one acres were planted, including 116 acres of replanting of larch areas. Parts of the moorland and around Elsi lake and Rhiwddolion were afforested, and a large area of old woodland near the village of Ro Wen, in the lower Conway valley, was treated with discretion with regard to choice of trees due to high amenity values.

A December gale blew down six acres of Sitka spruce and Douglas fir – planted in 1921 – in Maesnewyddion, extending the pocket-blown areas of 1953.

Radio communication was introduced and was to prove of in-estimable value in fire-check routines and management interchange of observations. For the first time, too, mist blowers for 24D and 2,4,5T weedkiller spraying were used. Sales of timber for the year exceeded ½ million cubic feet, with receipts in excess of £27,000.

DURING 1964, 282 acres were planted, involving areas as widespread as Mochdre, near Colwyn Bay, to the north, and Penmachno, to the south. The replanting of heavily-thinned larch areas continued, the principal species substituted being Sitka spruce. A forty acre nitrogen-deficient area of Sitka spruce at Penmachno was treated with urea, with favourable effects.

80

On the Lledr.

Camping on forest workers' holdings increased. Here was yet another aspect of public ingress. It was not unreasonable that people should want to camp within the forest confines for there were umpteen admirable locations and this particular fragment of the public, were, in the main, genuine open-air adherents with a respect for plantations and plantation life. Yet some kind of management plan for this ever mounting pressure was certainly required; here, too, the Forestry Commission could expect genuine response and forest consciousness from an expanding public seeking the quiet by-ways of the forest.

The mounted Rossplough was proving advantageous on short runs over relatively dry ground. A total of 480,509 hoppus feet of timber was harvested over the year.

IN 1965 two features of considerable interest involved fire protection and the forest centre. A new fire-observation hut was erected on Mynydd Deulyn, at 1,300 feet, between the lakes Geirionydd and Crafnant. This point covered the broad sweep of all the older-established Gwydyr plantations and many of the younger scattered outlying blocks. Radio communication with the forest control centre was started, and alignment bearings co-ordinated with the fire observation hut at Penmachno.

The Maesnewyddion forest-centre development was enlarged with the erection of oil and roads stores, a new office, and a canteen and toilet block. Electricity was installed throughout.

Weather-wise, two dates remain vividly in mind. The first was the night of 12th-13th December when a fearful concentration of rain – 5·9 inches – was recorded over 24 hours at Dolwyddelan. Second, a severe frost on 18th and 19th May caused extensive damage to developing lateral shoots of nearly all the principal species. Fortunately the leading shoots were not too seriously affected, though growth was set back. This was one of the bitterest spring frosts recorded over the years during late May, and stressed the threat of these incisive thrusts of nature at a critical time in a young tree's growth. The planting programme was a modest, widely scattered one of 251 acres, and again included certain felled larch areas. Two hundred and fourteen acres were afforested and 37 acres restocked.

Rabbits were everywhere on the increase; local outbreaks of myxomatosis seemingly had little effect. Two grey squirrels were observed, still confined to the Denbighshire side of the river Conway, and the campaign to arrest their progress westwards into the central forests concentration was intensified by the trappers.

In March of this year, Mr. James Griffiths, Secretary of State for Wales, visited the forest.

MANAGEMENT-WISE, 1966 was a significant year. The decision was taken to split the forest into three management units – Gwydyr, Machno and Lledr, though for fire protection co-ordination the forest retained its entity.

Two hundred and ninety-two acres were planted, 282 acres being new planting or afforestation and 10 acres restocking. Much of this programme involved Blaen-y-Cwm, at Penmachno, and 'checked' plantations on the Glyn – planted in 1931 and 1932. On parts of the heavily-thinned Japanese larch areas at Pencraig – planted 1923 – Leyland cypress were introduced as an undercrop.

IN 1967, the planting programme was much lower at 186 acres, containing 180 acres of new planting and six restocking. It was a year of quiet change, involving the introduction of a forest warden to deal with the mounting requests for forest visits by schools, colleges and study groups, and to plan and introduce recreational and amenity projects for the huge public influx. This factor was emerging as a crucial relationship, for more and more car drivers were seeking to use the forest roads and to get to the lakes within the forest.

A Forest Trail was prepared, signposted and a booklet produced. A total of 112 conducted parties were taken over the trail, and much use was made of it by local field study centres, hostels and outdoor pursuit centres, including the Central Council for Physical Recreation centre at Plas-y-Brenin, Capel Curig. A study of the environment of Snowdonia is incomplete without a forest visit.

The Director-General of the Forestry Commission visited Gwydyr specifically to review this public recreation aspect, and to inspect some of the work achieved; a ten-year working plan on the recreational, amenity and wild-life aspect of the forest was put in hand as a result of this visit.

THE 1968 PLANTING PROGRAMME realised a modest total of 152 acres, while 7 acres were re-afforested. On Mynydd Deulyn part of the very difficult exposed area was successfully ploughed. It proved to be a winter and spring of extreme weather vagaries, including a blanket fall of snow up to 10 inches in depth which mantled every branch of every tree, and remained unbroken for three days. A total of 4·42 inches of rain fell in 24 hours on 23rd March, accompanied by a gale force wind. Fortunately very little windblow was experienced though many road culverts were damaged by the excessive flow of water. A warm, dry spell occurred through most of July and early August and all river levels fell appreciably. A prolonged thunderstorm in May was accompanied by a spectacular forked and sheet lightning display. A record number of school, college and study groups visited the forest and were conducted over the forest trail.

FINALLY, THE YEAR 1969 saw celebrations for the Forestry Commission's fiftieth anniversary.

1970 WITNESSED the opening of the Forest Exhibition at Gwydyr Uchaf, close to Llanrwst. Planting continued at an average rate of 200 acres each year.

## THE FIFTH DECADE – CONCLUSIONS

### TIMBER PRODUCTION

Early higher altitude Japanese larch plantings were nearly all clear felled or heavily thinned by the end of the decade. Pulpwood material remained high as a harvesting product, but pitwood requirements tended to decrease.

A good price was obtained for the moss-collection rights within the forest, and also for the collection of Red cedar and cypress foliage.

### CLEANING

Much was accomplished in the detached derelict woodland blocks in the Conway valley area, for here coppice re-growth was strong and persistent. Some of the older areas (P. 35–45) still require some cleaning, particularly on checked sites.

### SMALLHOLDINGS

The run-down had persisted and most of the holding land had been resumed for planting.

### ROADS

A total of 135 miles of road served the forest and many of these sections opened up splendid vistas of plantation, foothill and mountain scenery.

### FIRE PROTECTION AND COMMUNICATIONS

The introduction of radio proved significant. This gave prompt and practical service and saved hours of investigation. Furthermore it united the lone patrolman or the mobile forester to a control centre, and reduced the psychological consternation derived from the first glimpse of the tell-tale smoke spiral so alarming for an alienated patrol in earlier years.

Forest roads, too, served as arteries for quick inspection and confirmation or otherwise of fire reports.

This subject is dealt with further in Chapter 8. It only remains to say that contact with schools, colleges, study groups, etc., who seek to learn something of forestry and the forest scene, cannot but instil a full sense of forest consciousness to a young generation and thus work to the good of forestry in the future. To a broader public who, by the end of the decade, were spreading into so many plantations alongside public roads, certain amenities such as picnic areas, viewpoints, etc., awakened their respect and appreciation to an important aspect of the Commission's function, namely good public relationship. It is certain that we shall benefit from this too, as the future unfolds.

Llyn Geirionydd.

## Chapter 8

# AMENITY, RECREATION, EDUCATION AND WILD-LIFE

Under the Forestry Act of 1967, the Forestry Commission is required to take account of the amenities of the countryside. These are within the visual amenity context. Since forest operations have a high influence on the aspect of the countryside a considerable moral responsibility falls on the Commission's staff. Their prime function is the establishment of forests and the production of timber, yet they must be constantly aware of the necessity to make the forest harmonise with the character of the countryside wherever possible. At Gwydyr, this awareness is made more acute by the popularity of the surrounding area; a forest operation, however small, becomes the cynosure of attention and comment. Some alien feature must, of necessity, intrude into the landscape somewhere –

86

log depots, creosoting tanks, etc., but so far as plantations are concerned, by careful selective choice and blending of species, restraint to any harsh clash with the environment has been achieved.

## PROVISION OF VISUAL AMENITY IN DIFFERENT FORMS

Probably more visitors pass through parts of Gwydyr forest than any other forest in Wales. Be they motorists, tourists, campers, walkers, excursionists or conducted parties — a multiplicity of tastes and aesthetic values embodied in a huge influx of people – the impact of the forest, in some measure, is appreciated and experienced in different ways. Then there is the resident population – quick to acclaim or denounce – and countless societies, organisations and authorities who feel they have a stake in what is good visual amenity and what is bad. Many profess to be able to supply means for all amenities, others genuinely desire to contribute some small helpful suggestions. All are involved. But it is the Forestry Commission staff who ultimately plan, undertake and maintain these visual amenity aspects and their achievements can be summarised into four distinct groups.

## THE NEAR PERSPECTIVE

This incorporates the establishment and maintenance of roadside broadleaved amenity belts or large groups of trees and would appeal primarily to the passing tourist or motorist.

## THE DISTANT PERSPECTIVE

Here attention is drawn to the retention of natural broadleaved species on steep slopes, crags, declivities among rocks and alongside screens, and small groups of oak, birch, ash, beech, etc., retained and incorporated within established plantations. Conifers have been carefully blended and follow natural features wherever possible, thus eliminating a 'hard' outline effect over much of the forest. This should appeal to all groups of people.

## ARBORETA AND FOREST PLOTS

This group comprises exotic and rare species not commonly grown for their commercial value. Arboreta play a distinctive role in the amenity feature since they contain many species which have been planted out in such a manner as to fit into the natural surroundings without obtruding their alien characteristics too severely against the environment. The full amenity potential of these species really lies in the years ahead – when individual form and outline will become more readily distinguishable. These arboreta exemplify the Commission's earnest endeavours to create and maintain a particular aspect of amenity that widens interest and promotes study.

87

Selected locations alongside public footpaths and minor roads throughout the forest, affording the visitor typical representative views of forest, valley and river.

So much for visual amenity; its long application at Gwydyr can be readily appreciated today. Aesthetically, it is debateable whether any other extensive forest area can combine productivity, charm and landscape-blending so successfully. The topography, admittedly, presents a wonderful backcloth to the forest setting – but it is the human contribution in the forest lay-out with which we are concerned. And surely this has been a remarkable achievement.

## THE RECREATIONAL ASPECT

Public pressure mounts and there is no stemming it. Significant in every way these selected remarks on the role of forests by the Chairman of the Forestry Commission, Mr. Leslie Jenkins, on the 12th November 1965, in his address at the 'Countryside in 1970' conference: 'It is probably true to say that the Countryside Commission, the Nature Conservancy and the Forestry Commission are the three public bodies within the Government family which are most closely concerned with the countryside and its use . . . in the Forestry Commission we mean to combine business with scenic beauty, and business with the pleasure of a public that is seeking it more and more in and around our forests . . . the countryside must be alive and dynamic. . . .'

Here, at Gwydyr, we are contributing a great deal to making it so and public response would seem to amply confirm this. We are fulfilling a really vital need in illustrating our work; furthermore we are gaining genuine adherents to the forest scene through the younger generation, which cannot but be advantageous to forestry in the years ahead. Because we must make people, and particularly young people, forest conscious, keenly aware of a heritage built up over fifty years, instil a forest tradition in them and give them a positive measure of the forests' worth as a social, aesthetic and economic inheritance.

At Gwydyr we have sited picnic areas and panoramic viewpoints alongside public footpaths and minor roads, and prepared forest trails. We have erected stone steps and rustic bridges, colour-coded footpaths. We are designating various usages for the lakes within the forest area (canoeing, wild-fowl breeding, etc.) as part of a ten-year working plan on amenity, recreation, education and wild life. We are signposting lakes and walks and labelling tree species.

In other words we are helping the public to make contact with us, we are leading them on to enjoy and appreciate the forest scene and to find relaxation within the plantations. This freedom to ramble along the trails and footpaths and enjoy fully all the concepts of a forest park places a solemn responsibility on the part of the public to observe a code of propriety towards growing trees and other living things encountered on their journeys. The majority exhibit the arts and niceties of decorum when they enter the forest; but what of the small minority who despoil notices, break fences and disturb walls? All too many are guilty of casting aside litter in some of its forms – paper, cartons, bottles, cans, packages. Abandoned litter – scourge of the countryside – who can possibly respect a woodland scene tarnished and fouled by extraneous objects cast aside in a moment's thoughtlessness? One cannot help quoting:

> 'Resemble not the slimy snail
> That leaves such filth along its trail,
> Let others see where you have been
> —— You've left the face of Nature clean.'

It seems to reflect an attitude of mind, perhaps unconsciously, but nevertheless constant, in the visitors to our forest parks. They are here today, they see, they appreciate, but they are gone tomorrow and their presence in our midst has been ruthlessly and sadly advertised.

We are planning ahead all the while to subscribe to forest recreation in as many aspects as possible within our available funds.

FOREST EDUCATION

Facilities are available for visiting schools, training colleges and study groups to utilise the forest trails and learn something about the problems and achievements of forestry. In the two years 1969–70 over 300 such parties were conducted over parts of the forest – nearly 7,000 people in all. We have good liaison with the Nature Conservancy, National Trust, many study and outdoor pursuit centres, Youth Hostels, etc. A forest museum is planned and coming into being. It is intended to mount permanent exhibits and displays in this, and to conduct lectures and talks on forestry to visiting groups. The general public is benefitting from this enterprise; literature is available for them and general information is dispersed.

To emphasise the great potential advantages of such a centre one has only to look, too, at the number of Youth Hostels, study centres, outdoor pursuit centres and physical recreational centres there are both within the forest and along its borders.

WILD LIFE

Certain of the small lakes and reservoirs within the forest are being set aside as wildfowl sites. On 6-inch Ordnance Survey sheets,

89

a resident mammal, bird and insect census is being compiled on the basis of locations and breeding.

## CONCLUSIONS

There are many associations of factors to take into consideration silviculturally, economically, aesthetically and ecologically. Some problems have no ready-made solution. One thing is certain, however. Our countryside is shrinking rapidly and its virgin charm distorted by the intrusion of extraneous structures.

This invasion, one presumes, is permanent; we are all-too-familiar with pylons on the skyline and hill slopes, concrete edifices in the dales and cwms. It is exceptional nowadays to find a few square miles of genuine, unspoilt countryside within any county.

The formation of forest parks and nature reserves is our last retreat; they are the final haunt of flora and fauna natural to our island nation. The Forestry Commission are the largest landowners in the country and as such have an added responsibility other than growing timber. Their forest parks provide silviculture, recreation, education, visual and practical amenity, nature conservation, hill farming – a rich heritage for the young and a wealth of repose for the elderly, and a real, positive practical demonstration of multiple land-use.

We are proud of Gwydyr. This massive creation, this achievement – nourished and unfolded over fifty years of endeavour – has next to no shortcomings in the aesthetic sense. It is an exhibit worthy of the highest respect, for even if there are practical silvicultural imperfections and frailties, just contemplate the landscape spread over and across the steep valley slopes and broad sweep of broken upland plateau. Heed the blend of shade in the tree species, the conformity of plantation to the configuration of the ground, the open 'alps' of green field scattered through the forest, the gentle touch of broad-leaved trees among the conifers. Unsightly? Artificial? Regimented? Surely not; for here is grandeur, economical grandeur, set amidst and against some of the most formidable and inhospitable afforestation locations imaginable.

The Forestry Commission was conceived almost immediately after one world war, it endured a second. All of you can now enjoy the fruits of five decades of endeavour, and trial and accomplishment – your heritage is here, alongside you.

All that is required is the understanding, support and participation of the public in preserving these vital beauties we have so disparagingly inherited and zealously created. In the words of Henry van Dyke:

> 'He that planteth a tree is the servant of God.
> He  provideth a kindness for many generations, and
> Faces that he hath not seen, shall bless him.'

# APPENDIX I

## OBSERVATIONS ON TREE SPECIES GROWN

SCOTS PINE

During the early years this species was selected for gorse and gorse/grass sites on dry, rocky knolls. Later it was introduced on heather-gorse associations with promising results, but since 1937 it has not been planted extensively on exposed sites due to its inhibited growth in high rainfall areas and its propensity to snowbreak.

Really excellent tree form can be seen on areas at Penrallt Uchaf, planted in 1924 on an initial vegetation complex of gorse, bracken and grass. Here, establishment was rapid and uniform.

On 1930 planting areas on the Glyn, response has not been so good, though here a long check period ensued on heather/*Molinia*/ *Eriophorum* complexes. At Pandora, planted during 1929, there are many good groups in an otherwise patchy plantation on a very inhospitable site.

Since 1964 Scots pine has been frequently used in mixture with Sitka spruce on ploughed heather ground, and this association has proved notably successful on the Bwlch (1949) and Bwlch-y-Maen (1950).

The best volume figures appear to be produced on south, south-west and south-east aspects, on sites carrying moderate gorse/grass/ bracken vegetation.

CORSICAN PINE

Restricted planting due to (a) incidence of the *Brunchorstia* fungus at high levels and under heavy rainfall conditions, (b) unsuitability of most of the sites.

Three well established belts on Diosgydd – planted in 1921, Coed-y-Wern (planted 1923) and on rock outcrops on the Lledr valley show this species to best advantage.

On Diosgydd, on a southerly aspect with good natural drainage, growth has been excellent and uniform. Initially, on this location, there was dense gorse competition to contend with.

At present the volume per acre stands only a little below that of adjacent Douglas fir on this site and tree form is exceptionally good.

LODGEPOLE PINE

This species began to be used on a fairly extensive scale in 1929, on a variety of the poorest ground on the plateau areas, where it was selected to beat-up failed spruce plantations on the poorest peats and on rocky gorse/heather/*Molinia* knolls.

*Plate 24.* Broad sweep of plantations on south side of Llugwy.

*Plate 25.* Llyn Geirionydd, view near picnic site.

*Plate 26.* The Llanrwst by-road climbs to cross uplands north of Ugly House.

Two conclusions can certainly be drawn with regard to this species:

(1) It is the most tolerant and reliable of all the pines for the poorest ground conditions.
(2) It will resist drought on thin soils over rock.

Generally, Lodgepole pine is very adaptable to a wide range of plateau sites and has developed uniformly, i.e. Diosgydd Uchaf (planted 1931) and Alltwen mountain (planted 1929). On pure heather sites it has not tended to maintain uniformity consistently; north, north-west and west aspects would appear to illustrate better tree form and a reliable growth rate.

As a nurse species for Sitka spruce particularly, it has assisted establishment on the poorest possible areas which would otherwise have remained in a condition of severe and prolonged check.

EUROPEAN LARCH

Planted from 1921 to 1936 and then discontinued. This species was used mostly on the higher valley slopes previously supporting a timber crop, and occasionally on the lower slopes where the ground was considered too soft for Douglas fir. It was never successful.

On higher ground its growth rate was too slow, its form sickly and misshapen, and there was evidence of much canker. The below-average growth rate contributed to high and protracted weeding costs.

During 1937 the decision was taken to abandon further European larch planting at Gwydyr, and to substitute with Japanese larch. Much heavy thinning of the European larch plantations was necessary and enrichment resorted to. With the removal of the malformed trees the survivors have responded well and promise the formation of a useful final crop.

JAPANESE LARCH

Consistently used since the formation of the forest, though not on any extensive scale. Quick and easy to establish on the sheltered sites where weed growth is heaviest. It has been planted on the plateau lands where bracken flushes flourished, but has not responded well. On gorse sites it has failed completely and is unreliable on wet soils. Perhaps we expected too much of it in the earlier years, and since 1958 most of the upland plantations have been clear felled or heavily thinned. The species has not been overlooked on two scores: (a) Amenity grounds; (b) Fire protection needs, both of high significance on the majority of Gwydyr's locations.

Japanese larch has always been a fast starter, but has tended to

Douglas firs by Mymbyr Bridge, Capel Curig.

'tail off' in height growth and volume increment after some thirty years and be overtaken by some more valuable species such as Douglas fir and Sitka spruce. Generally south and south-east aspects favour this species.

Regularly planted on the steep, boulder-clad lower valley slopes of old woodland areas, where it established well, and quickly suppressed gorse and coppice competition; due to its early shade-bearing capacities it has been used consistently too, to underplant scrub areas.

Its reaction to the chosen sites has been favourable, for it was realised from the outset that the species was vulnerable to wind and snow damage on the steep, broken slopes. Some windthrow has occurred; there were too, some years, when due to financial stringency many areas could not be cleaned thoroughly, resulting in a lower stocking than normal.

Much staking was resorted to in the early years to redress wind buffeting and bending, and many Douglas fir areas were checked by *Adelges* insects in their formative period. The ill-effects of *Adelges* attack gradually disappeared, however, and most plantations have grown uniformly. In 1949–50 heart staining was observed on third thinnings removed from Diosgydd (planted in 1921).

Despite these minor encroachments, Douglas fir is generally very successful and forms some of the finest plantations on the valley slopes.

SITKA SPRUCE

The principle species at Gwydyr. Used extensively from 1921 onwards over a wide range of sites from sheltered felled woodland to the most exposed of plateau locations. It failed completely only on the poorest peats on the rocky knolls.

Remarkably it has remained relatively free of intense Honey Fungus infection on old woodland sites. On non-peat slopes, plantation development has been patchy where there was shallow soil, but on exposed *Molinia*-heath vegetation complexes it has grown consistently well. Pure heather areas caused severe check for many years, and in gullies and hollows supporting dominant *Molinia*, Sitka suffered severely at times from late spring frosts.

Despite its prolonged struggle to get established over many of the most inhospitable sites at Gwydyr – for that matter on some of the most difficult areas anywhere in the country – and for three decades before the onset of mechnical means to accomplish superior site preparation prior to planting (thus assisting in favourable establishment conditions), the species has sustained its role as the most valuable pioneer crop over a wide range of upland vegetation complexes.

## NORWAY SPRUCE

During the first decade, and for half of the second, a compatible companion-at-arms to Sitka on many sites, sharing old woodland locations and much of the plateau land. After 1932, however, its use was restricted on many of the latter areas.

Norway spruce has been very successful on bracken/grass land which contained too high a proportion of wet patches to make Japanese larch an altogether safe choice. On the more sheltered peat slopes of *Juncus* and *Molinia* it has succeeded, too, but on the flat *Molinia* zones and on *Myrica/Molinia* associations its response has been slow.

Throughout the latter years of the 30's there was an acute shortage of Sitka spruce, resulting in much substitution by Norway on many plateau land sites. On gorse/heather/*Molinia* peats on rock ridges and outcrops, Norway spruce settled to a long and complete check and became badly blasted through exposure. After 1937 Norway spruce was prohibited on high heather ground and *Molinia*, if intermixed with inferior indicators such as cross-leaved heather.

## WESTERN HEMLOCK

Confined to relatively small areas since 1927 – when it was first introduced in Miner's Bridge plantation – this species has shown a high potential on old woodland areas, notably in Miner's Bridge, Glyn Lledr and Soflen. Two small blocks on the Glyn (planted in 1930), both on very rocky ground and planted through the cover of old oak on fairly exposed sites, display fine stem form for such an altitude (over 700 feet). Ostensibly the species is fairly adaptable and is a good amenity tree; its potential on upland boulder-strewn terrain under scrub oak/birch would seem to be reasonably high. It has succeeded well on all the selected sites, particularly on south and south-east facing slopes.

## WESTERN RED CEDAR

Limited plantations have been established on old woodland sites, incurring certain Honey Fungus risks. In 1930 a small area was planted on the Glyn on a rocky site and under some difficulties; later, in 1932, plantations were formed at Diosgydd followed by Dolgarrog (1935) and Craig Forys (1936), all of them on bouldery, dense scrub slopes. At Dolgarrog there has been a high mortality rate due to Honey Fungus since 1947.

At Diosgydd and on the Glyn, however, tree form is very good and consistent growth-rate has been maintained. South and south-east aspects are quite the most favourable.

### LAWSON CYPRESS

Planting of this species has been very limited in extent. A very good plot at Diosgydd – planted in 1932 – can be observed, and here the trees are not as prone to stem forking as was thought likely. There is evidence that it will succeed on some plateau sites carrying gorse/heather mixtures.

### GRAND SILVER FIR

First planted in 1927 at Miner's Bridge and has responded magnificently. There seems to be appreciable loss of vigour when planted under shade, though the species has been confined to relatively limited areas throughout the forest, so far. An attractive amenity tree and a large volume producer for its age, grand fir has not, as yet, proved susceptible to Honey Fungus or heart rot.

### NOBLE SILVER FIR

This species has not been planted on any appreciable scale so far, the first plot being established in 1927, in Miner's Bridge plantation. Growth-rate has been slower than for Grand fir and crop development is more uneven.

A high-elevation trial plot was established at Ty'n-y-Cwm in 1951, and it would appear now that Noble fir can succeed tolerably well on difficult gorse/heather locations under fairly exposed conditions.

A considerable variety of other species is found throughout the forest, either in the arboretae or in small groups or as single specimens at specified points.

# APPENDIX 2

## STATEMENT OF FOREST LAND
## TOTAL AND USAGE, 1969

*NOTE*

Since 1966 Gwydyr has been split into three separate forests, namely Gwydyr, Lledr and Machno. This history, however, embraces the whole of the original Gwydyr area and these figures combine the three unit totals, at the last available date.

| TOTAL FOREST AREA (at 30th March, 1969) | UNDER PLANTATIONS | TO BE PLANTED | AGRICULTURAL AND MOUNTAIN LAND |
|---|---|---|---|
| 20,112 acres | 14,045 acres | 1,003 acres | 5,064 acres |
| Conifer species (rounded) | 13,100 acres (95%) | | |
| Broadleaved species | 600 acres (4%) | | |
| Mixed species | 200 acres (1%) | | |

*Species acreage*

| | |
|---|---|
| Sitka spruce | 5,600 acres |
| Norway spruce | 1,720 acres |
| Japanese larch | 1,835 acres |
| Douglas fir | 1,656 acres |
| Scots pine | 830 acres |
| Lodgepole pine | 330 acres |
| European larch | 274 acres    Most plantations now underplanted. |
| Corsican pine | |
| Western hemlock | |
| Western red cedar | |
| Silver firs | 1,800 acres |
| Lawson cypress | |
| Broadleaved species | |
| Minor species and mixtures | |

# APPENDIX 3

## SELECTED CONIFEROUS TREES FOUND IN THE FOREST

| Scientific name | English name | Country of origin |
|---|---|---|
| *ABIES–THE SILVER FIRS* | | |
| Abies grandis | Grand silver fir | Western North America |
| Abies procera | Noble fir | Western North America |
| Abies cephalonica | Grecian fir | Mountains of Greece |
| Abies nordmanniana | Caucasian fir | Caucasus |
| Abies alba | Common silver fir | Europe |
| Abies veitchii | Veitch fir | Japan |
| Abies concolor | Colorado fir | Colorado, U.S.A. |
| Abies magnifica | Red fir | Western North America |
| Abies lasiocarpa | Alpine fir | Western North America |
| Abies concolor variety lowiana | Low fir | Western North America |
| Abies pinsapo | Spanish fir | Mountains of Spain |
| | | |
| *PINUS–THE PINES* | | |
| Pinus sylvestris | Scots pine | Europe, inc. Britain |
| Pinus nigra var calabrica | Corsican pine | Europe, inc. Corsica |
| Pinus contorta | Lodgepole pine | W.N. America |
| Pinus radiata | Monterey pine | California |
| Pinus ponderosa | Western yellow pine | W.N. America |
| Pinus strobus | Weymouth pine | E.N. America |
| Pinus mugo | Mountain pine | Europe (Alps) |
| Pinus peuke | Macedonian pine | Balkan Mountains |
| Pinus monticola | Western white pine | W.N. America |
| Pinus pinaster | Maritime pine | Mediterranean |
| Pinus coulteri | Big-cone pine | California |
| Pinus attenuata | Knob-cone pine | Oregon, U.S.A. |
| | | |
| *PICEA–THE SPRUCES* | | |
| Picea sitchensis | Sitka spruce | W. North America |
| Picea abies | Norway spruce | Europe |
| Picea glauca | White spruce | North America |
| Picea omorika | Serbian spruce | South-west Serbia |
| Picea jezoensis | Yeddo spruce | Japan |
| Picea morinda | Himalayan spruce | West Himalaya |
| Picea brachytyla | Sargent spruce | China |
| Picea asperata | Dragon spruce | China |
| Picea orientalis | Oriental spruce | Asia Minor |
| Picea likiangensis | Li-Kiang spruce | China |
| Picea engelmannii | Engelmann's spruce | W.N. America |
| Picea mariana | Black spruce | N. America |
| | | |
| *LARIX–THE LARCHES* | | |
| Larix decidua | European larch | Europe |
| Larix Kaempferi | Japanese larch | Japan |
| Larix eurolepis | Hybrid larch | |

## PSEUDOTSUGA–DOUGLAS FIR

| | | |
|---|---|---|
| Pseudotsuga menziesii | Douglas fir | W.N. America |

## TSUGA-HEMLOCKS

| | | |
|---|---|---|
| Tsuga heterophylla | Western hemlock | W.N. America |

## CEDRUS–THE CEDARS

| | | |
|---|---|---|
| Cedrus libani | Cedar of Lebanon | Syrian Mountains |
| Cedrus atlantica | Atlas cedar | North Africa |
| Cedrus deodora | Deodar | Himalaya |

## SEQUOIA, etc.

| | | |
|---|---|---|
| Sequoia sempervirens | Redwood | California |
| Sequoiadendron giganteum | Mammoth tree | California |

## CHAMAECYPARIS, etc.–THE CYPRESSES

| | | |
|---|---|---|
| Chamaecyparis lawsoniana | Lawson cypress | W.N. America |
| Cupressocyparis leylandii | Leyland cypress | (Hybrid developed at Leighton, Montgomery) |

## THUJA

| | | |
|---|---|---|
| Thuja plicata | Western red cedar | W.N. America |
| Thuja orientalis | Chinese arbor-vitae | China |

## CRYPTOMERIA

| | | |
|---|---|---|
| Cryptomeria japonica | Japanese cedar | Japan |

# APPENDIX 4

## SELECTED BROADLEAVED TREES FOUND IN THE FOREST

| Scientific name | English name | Country of origin |
|---|---|---|
| Aesculus hippocastanum | Horse chestnut | Asia Minor |
| Castanea sativa | Sweet chestnut | Greece |
| Quercus robur | Oak, Pedunculate | Britain |
| Quercus petraea | Oak, Sessile | |
| Fraxinus excelsior | Ash | Britain |
| Acer pseudoplatanus | Sycamore | Europe |
| Fagus sylvatica | Beech | Britain |
| Betula pendula | Birch | Britain |
| Populus (species) | Poplars (various) | Europe and America |
| Prunus spinosa | Blackthorn | Britain |
| Prunus avium | Gean (Wild cherry) | Britain |
| Sorbus aucuparia | Mountain ash (Rowan) | Britain |
| Crataegus monogyna | Hawthorn | Britain |
| Sambucus nigra | Elder | Britain |
| Ulmus glabra | Elm (Wych) | Britain |
| Ulmus procera | Elm (English) | England |
| Alnus glutinosa | Alder | Britain |
| Carpinus betulus | Hornbeam | Britain |
| Salix species | Willow | Britain |
| Quercus rubra | American Red oak | U.S.A. |
| Nothofagus obliqua and Nothofagus procera | Southern beeches | Chile |

# APPENDIX 5

## WELSH PLANTATION AND PLACE-NAMES TRANSLATED

| *WELSH* | *ENGLISH* |
|---|---|
| Coed Maesnewyddion | New-fields wood |
| Hafod yr Ewen (ywen) | Sheiling (summer pasturage dwelling) of the yew |
| Llyn Sarnau | Lake of the causeways |
| Bryn y Fawnog | Hill of the peat bog |
| Ty'n Llwyn | House in the grove |
| Llyn Bodgynydd | Lake of the huntsman's dwelling |
| Mynydd Bwlch yr Haiarn | Mountain of the pass of iron |
| Llyn Crafnant | Lake of the valley of garlic |
| Cefn Manllwyd | Hill (ridge) of the grey stone |
| Coed Ffrith Sian | Wood of Jane's rough hillside – grazing |
| Coed Clogwyn Gwlyb | Wood of the wet precipice |
| Coed Pant y Caseg | Mare's dell wood |
| Coed Fuches-las | Wood of the grey/blue herd |
| Coedmawr | Big wood |
| Llety | Lodge |
| Coed Cae Huddygl | Wood of the sooty field |
| Talar Gerwyn | Gerwyn's headland (of ploughed field) |
| Bwlch y Maen | Pass of the stones |
| Glasgwm | Green valley |
| Cwm Celyn | Valley of the holly |
| Cwm Dreiniog | Thorny valley |
| Hafod Gwenllian | Gwenllian's summer sheiling |
| Hafod Ffrith-isaf | Sheiling of the lower hill-slope |
| Llechweddhafod | Hill slope of the shieling |
| Gwyndy | White house |
| Hafod Dwyryd | Sheiling of the river Dwyryd |
| Bryn Engan | Engan's hill |
| Wyddfyd | Honeysuckle |
| Craig Forys | Morris's rock |
| Coed Creigiau | Wood of the rocks |
| Coed-y-Wern | Wood of the alders |
| Gallt-yr-Ysfa | Slope of the mountain grazing |
| Cae Dibyn | Field precipice |
| Fedw Hendre | Birches of the old settlement |
| Coed Cynhelier | The hidden wood |
| Coed Soflen | The wood of stubbles |
| Rhiwddolion | Slope of the wanderers |
| Clogwyn Cyrau | Precipice of the corner |
| Llyn Bychan | The little lake |
| Llyn-y-Lparc | The lake of the enclosed fields |
| Llyn Ty'n-y-Mynydd | Lake of the house on the mountain |

# APPENDIX 6

## PLACES OF INTEREST IN AND NEAR THE FOREST

The forest itself, and its environs, are set amidst an area of great natural beauty. Minor public roads and many footpaths cross the sprawling plantation massif, affording the visitor a countless number and variety of views. The fascination of these scenic splendours is endless.

But there are, too, many distinctive places to visit – castles, churches, dwellings, bridges, etc., of historical and architectural interest – all either within the forest boundary or a brief car-run away.

This list details such places, with lakes and waterfalls, which are of special appeal within this rampart of natural beauty.

*Castles, Churches, Historical Buildings, etc.*

| | |
|---|---|
| Conway Castle | Built by Edward I between 1283–1289 |
| Dolwyddelan Castle | Keep dates from 2nd half of 12th century. |
| Gwydyr Castle | |
| Gwydyr Uchaf Chapel | Built 1673 |
| St. Michael's Church, Betws-y-Coed | |
| Llanrychwyn Church | 6th century |
| Dolwyddelan Church | |
| Ugly House (Ty-Hyll) | |
| Fedw deg | |
| Ty Mawr, Gwibernant | Birthplace of Bishop Morgan, who first translated the Bible into Welsh. |
| Ty Hwnt i'r bont (Llanrwst) | The house beyond the bridge. |

*Burial Chambers*

Capel Garmon, early Bronze Age.

*Lakes – Llynau in Welsh*

Llyn Elsi
Llyn y Parc
Llyn Geirionydd (with monument to Taliesin)
Llyn Crafnant
Llyn Goddion-duon
Llyn Cowlyd
Llyn Bodgynydd
Llyn Bodgynydd Bach
Llynau Mymbyr

*Waterfalls, Bridges, Beauty Spots*

Swallow Falls
Mare's-tail Falls
Conway Falls
Machno Falls
Beaver Pool
Fairy Glen
Pont y Pair bridge (Betws-y-Coed)
Waterloo Bridge
Llanrwst Bridge (1636)
Trefriw Pumproom and Baths

# APPENDIX 7

## FORESTRY TERMS EXPLAINED

AFFORESTATION
: The establishment of a tree crop on land not previously supporting timber.

BASAL AREA
: The area of the cross-section of a tree stem at breast height.

BEATING-UP
: The replacing of plants which have succumbed in the initial planting.

CANOPY
: The screen or cover formed by the crowns of the trees in a plantation.

CLEANING
: The removal or control of weed species in a planted crop.

COMPARTMENT
: A unit of area within the forest permanently defined for purposes of description and record.

COPPICE
: A stem that has sprung from a stump and not from seed.

ECOLOGY
: The study of plant life in relation to its environment.

FIRE LINE
: A strip of ground which is kept free of inflammable vegetation, to limit the spread of fire or form a point of attack against it.

FROST LIFT
: The lifting of nursery plants, or small plants newly established, out of the ground due to alternate freezing and thawing of the soil.

FROST HOLLOW
: An area, often limited in size, in which frosts are more frequent or more severe than in the locality generally.

GROUND VEGETATION
: Small plants (other than young planted trees) growing on the forest floor, such as grass, ferns, heather, bog-myrtle, etc.

HUMUS
: Organic matter in the soil, in process of decomposition.

INCREMENT
: The rate at which a tree or tree crop increases with age. Increment may be measured in volume, height or diameter.

| | |
|---|---|
| KNOT | A mark in timber caused by the inclusion of the base of a branch in the wood of a tree stem. |
| LEACHING | The washing away of substances by the percolation of water through the soil. |
| LIMITING FACTOR | That factor in the environment, which, owing to its unfavourable condition, has the greatest effect in limiting growth in a particular case. |
| LITTER | The dead leaves, twigs and other debris shed by the trees and other vegetation and lying on the forest floor. |
| NATURAL REGENERATION | The formation of a new forest crop by seed shed naturally on the ground. |
| PAN | A hard layer in the soil at some distance below the surface, caused by the accumulation of mineral and organic substances washed down from the upper layers. |
| PRECIPITATION | The water which reaches the earth in the form of rain, snow, hail, hoar-frost, etc. |
| PRUNING | The artificial cutting-off of branches from the stems of trees. |
| ROTATION | The period elapsing between the formation of a plantation and its final harvesting. |
| SHADE-BEARING OR SHADE-TOLERANT | A species capable of surviving and developing in shade. |
| THINNING | The cutting-out of selected trees from a plantation to gain a harvest and improve the growth and quality of the remainder. |
| THINNING CYCLE | The time which elapses between successive thinnings on the same area. |
| TURF PLANTING | A method of planting, employed chiefly on peaty soils, by which turves are cut from drains and used as mounds for the plants. |
| UNDERPLANTING | The introduction of a second crop of trees under one already established. |
| WORKING PLAN | A document which sets forth the aims of the management and the scheme of operations by which it is hoped to attain them. |

# APPENDIX 8

## MAMMALS AND BIRDS FOUND IN THE FOREST

MAMMALS

Hedgehog
Mole
Common Shrew
Long-Eared Bat
Fox
Badger
Stoat

Weasel
Polecat
Rabbit
Brown Hare
Mountain Hare
Red Squirrel
Grey Squirrel (local)

REPTILES

Adder
Grass Snake

Lizard
Slow-worm

PRINCIPAL BIRDS

Raven
Rook
Jackdaw
Jay
Black Grouse
Red Grouse
Finches (various)
Sparrowhawk
Tawny Owl
Woodpecker (Green and
    Great Spotted)
Little Owl
Buzzard
Tree-Creeper
Blackbird
Thrush
Robin
Little Grebe
Mallard

Coot
Teal
Black-headed Gull
    (Late April–Early June)
Stonechat
Woodcock
Tits (various)
Wood Pigeon
Skylark
Curlew
Magpie
Moorhen
Nuthatch
Nightjar
Pheasant
Pipit (Meadow, Tree)
Redstart
Wagtail (Pied, Yellow)

*Printed in England for Her Majesty's Stationery Office by Swindon Press Ltd., Swindon, Wilts.*
Dd 501963 K56 Gp469

# FORESTRY COMMISSION GUIDES

ARGYLL FOREST PARK. 35p.
BEDGEBURY, KENT (National Pinetum and Forest Plots)
 *Short Guide.* 4p.
CAMBRIAN FORESTS. (*Under revision*)
FORESTS OF CENTRAL AND SOUTHERN SCOTLAND (*Booklet
 No.* 25) 62½p.
THE NEW FORESTS OF DARTMOOR (*Booklet No.* 10) 12½p.
DEAN FOREST AND WYE VALLEY (Forest Park) 32½p.
GLAMORGAN FORESTS. 25p.
GLEN MORE FOREST PARK (*Cairngorms*). 42½p.
GLEN TROOL FOREST PARK (*Galloway*). 30p.
KILMUN ARBORETUM AND FOREST PLOTS. 10p.
NEW FOREST. 35p.
FORESTS OF NORTH-EAST SCOTLAND. 25p.
NORTH YORKSHIRE FORESTS. 37½p.
QUEEN ELIZABETH FOREST PARK *Short Guide.* 5p.
SNOWDONIA FOREST PARK. 32½p.
SNOWDONIA FOREST PARK *Short Guide.* 2½p.
FORESTRY IN THE WEALD (*Booklet No.* 22). 17½p.
WESTONBIRT ARBORETUM. 4p.
WESTONBIRT IN COLOUR. 10p.

*Also*
FOREST PARKS (*Booklet No.* 6). 17½p.
KNOW YOUR CONIFERS (*Booklet No.* 15). 30p.
FORESTRY IN THE LANDSCAPE (*Booklet No.* 18). 17½p.
KNOW YOUR BROADLEAVES (*Booklet No.* 20). 75p.
PUBLIC RECREATION IN NATIONAL FORESTS (*Booklet
 No.* 21). 45p.
FORESTRY IN THE BRITISH SCENE (*Booklet No.* 24). 50p.


Postage extra on all prices.


*Obtainable from*
HER MAJESTY'S STATIONERY OFFICE
*at the addresses on the back cover
or through any bookseller*

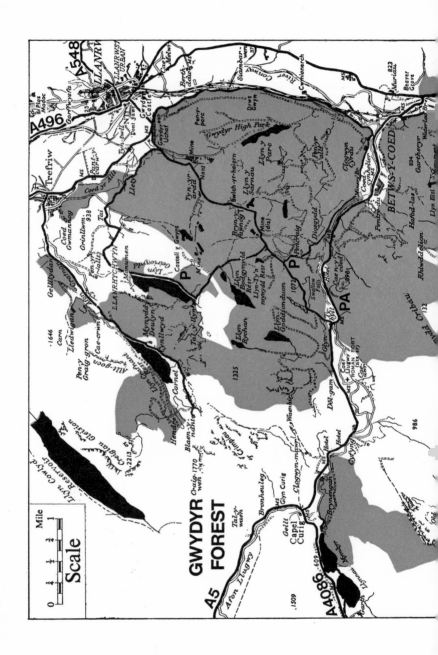